/ Visual Literature Criticism /
A New Collection

Edited by Richard Kostelanetz

Southern Illinois University Press
Carbondale and Edwardsville
Feffer & Simons, Inc.
London and Amsterdam

Library of Congress Cataloging in Publication Data

Main entry under title:

Visual literature criticism.

   Bibliography: p.
   1. Visual literature—History and criticism—
Addresses, essays, lectures. I. Kostelanetz,
Richard.
PN56.V54V5   809.1   79-18457
ISBN 0-8093-0950-5

Dedicated by the editor to William H. Goetzmann and William Stott

Visual forms—lines, colors, proportions, etc.—are just as capable of *articulation,* i.e., of complex combination, as words. But the laws that govern this sort of articulation are altogether different from the laws of syntax that govern language. The most radical difference is that *visual forms are not discursive.* They do not present their constituents successively, but simultaneously, so that relations determining a visual structure are grasped in one act of vision.

—Suzanne Langer, *Philosophy in a New Key* (1942).

For years, many years, poets have intensively and efficiently exploited the spatial possibilities of poetry.

Verses ending halfway on the page, verses having a wider or a narrower margin, verses being separated from the following one by a bigger or smaller space—all this is exploitation of space.

But only the so-called concrete, or, later, visual poetry, has openly declared this.

A book of 500 pages, or of 100 pages, or even of 25, wherein all the pages are similar, is a boring book, as a book, no matter how thrilling the content of the words of the text printed on the pages might be.

—Ulises Carrion, "The New Art of Making Books" (1975).

Contemporary works of fiction are often experienced with a certain anxiety, not because they threaten to extinguish the short story or the novel as recognizable genres, but because they challenge the traditional bases of both cultural and aesthetic judgments.

—Raymond Federman, "Fiction Today or the Pursuit of Non-Knowledge" (1977).

The vocabulary of criticism will have to include, if it is to come to terms with the meaning of these operations, such words as permutation, conversion, and rotation. It will have to consider the meaning and value of operations such as differentiation, amplification, and reduction.

—William S. Wilson, "Focus, Meter, and Operations in Poetry," *Stony Book* (1969).

PREFACE

This is, as far as I can discern, the first symposium of *criticism* of visual literature in English. Critical consciousness of this strain of literary art has so far been more pronounced both in Germany and Italy, where such symposia have appeared in the past; the English-speaking countries are visibly retarded in this respect. The project began a year ago with an invitation addressed to everyone I knew to be interested in the subject. This invitation read, in part, "Visual literature is tentatively defined as language structures whose principal means of coherence and/or enhancement are visual, rather than semantic or syntactical; or images, with or without words, that function like a poem or a fiction or an essay." In mind were visual poetry, visual fiction, conceptually unified photograph books, illuminated manuscripts, most "artist's books," etc. Cautiously, I added, "This definition is subject to revision, if challenged by the essays themselves."

This symposium, I continued, "will include both longer pieces and short reviews. Nothing will be assigned or commissioned. The length of the issue will depend upon the available material. Critical analyses will be preferred to impressionistic responses; disinterested evaluations to florid appreciations. Previously published material will be considered only if it is incorporated into a fresh context." Otherwise, the invitation was meant to be as open, and as inviting, as possible.

Nonetheless, some people misread the instructions and sent visual literature, some of which was quite good; but only *criticism* would, for better and worse, be the subject of this collection. Others sent laudatory reviews, including one of me; these, alas, had to be returned. My assumption in doing this project is that the development of a substantial critical tradition can be as important to avant-garde writing as the appearance of persuasive anthologies. In one of the sagest passages of modernist criticism, Hugh Kenner noted,

> There is no substitute for critical tradition: a continuum of understanding, early commenced.... Precisely because William Blake's contemporaries did not know what to make of him, we do not know either, though critic after critic appeases our sense of obligation to his genius by reinventing him....
> In the 1920s, on the other hand, *something* was immediately made of *Ulysses* and *The Waste Land,* and our comfort with both works after 50 years, including our ease at allowing for their age, seems derivable from the fact that they have never been ignored.

The essays collected here should also show that criticism about visual literature can be as intelligent as that about rhymed verse or realistic fiction. On the other hand, the essays are as various in approach and style as the works they describe, for the criticism of visual literature is no more monolithic than the literature itself. Several contri-

butors chose to write about themselves, if only to raise general esthet-
ic and critical issues that might otherwise go unnoticed. A final implication of this symposium is that the discussion is scarcely over;
there are problems here to challenge the strongest critical minds.

I am particularly grateful to William L. Fox for commissioning this
project and to the dedicatees for rescuing me, hospitably and pleas-
antly for a semester, from the slough of New York despond.

Richard Kostelanetz
New York, New York
11 July, 1978

INTRODUCTION

Once time and space, action and thought, became captured in writing, literature inevitably became involved with material substances: ink, pen, papyrus, stone, paper, etc. Literature remains a communication of the logical and expressive power of language, but to varying degrees it is also a vehicle for the communication of uniquely visual qualities.

Printed literature is becoming electronic literature: nonphysical, alphanumeric symbols mixed with other images that are displayed as light and can be stored, distributed, and enjoyed anywhere at any time.

To even the casual observer it would be clear that no satisfactory definition could embrace all the forms of visual poetry, variously identified as technopaegnia, pattern-poems, concretism, spatialism, and so forth. Yet what holds true for all of visual poetry is that to achieve its full effect, language *must be visually perceived.*

Creative jongleurs of the late Middle Ages and the Renaissance also liked the *vers batelés,* or juggled verses. This practice consisted of writing lines which could be read in more than one direction.

In the case of visual poems which are primarily visual and only lesserly textual—the verbally poetic visual piece—a similar metamorphosis occurs: the verbal aspect becomes transcendent to its visual embodiment, and a kinetic thrust becomes possible in a way that very few visual art works can have.

It is easy for us to see how the syncretism of a [Giordano] Bruno fits well with the formal syncretism of recent visual poetry and parallel art forms —conceptual art, Fluxus performances and Happenings, for instance—and indicates the synchronic appropriateness of it.

For Mallarmé, particularly in his later poetry, the doctrine of the purification of the word implies a conscious rejection of all the words (and ideas) that are customarily associated with that word—and, as a corollary, it equally implies a search for other words that bear no immediately obvious relationship to the word in question.

In the visual poetry movement, which claims Mallarmé as an influence (particularly for the typographical experiments of *Un coup de dés*), syntax often disappears entirely, being replaced by spatial relationships which provide the structure traditionally created by syntax.

This closeness between the word as composition and representation, between what it does and what it wears (its shape or visual uniqueness), was something felt throughout Antiquity.

Putting it another way, Optatian, by wedding the new and untried to the old in such a way that new signs and forms take root, in-forming the old verse forms and meters, without doing violence to traditional ways, to traditional language and art (i.e., culture), both reveals and reflects the exact nature of Constantine's imperium, which attempted to bridge and unify both classical past and oncoming Judeochristian universalism with its attendant, imperial-theological rhetoric.

That poem is most complete when it unequivocally points to objects, ideas, events, relations; leaves nothing more to be desired; contains nothing which it does not reveal; and thereby drives us toward the object which it designates.

We are dealing here not so much with words as with "coefficients," "exponents," or "linguistic tools," which have use value rather than signification. Brackets. Arrows. Shafts. Each has no signifying power that we can isolate, but, when joined together in a verbal chain, make unquestionable sense.

Such a verbo-visual system [as the *I Ching*] seems simultaneously contemporary and primitive because its purpose is not the expression of King Wen's private agony, but the ritual of self-discovery for the reader. The experience, then, seems to change the state of consciousness of the listener, giving him access to parts of his mind he does not use in everyday life.

In many of [!an Hamilton] Finlay's works, the poetic activity consists largely of establishing such a context, the "field" (sometimes literally) of "being a poem." Within this field, one concise image—often reduced to a single proper name, number, or fact—can extend its significance in a witty and controlled play among the levels evoked by the context.

If ever there were a writer who needed a visual form for his fiction to succeed, it would have to be Raymond Federman. . . .Once rolling, he won't stop, having told the same story four times over: . . . .And each book is a visual and narrative joy—a story which can be told and retold as many times as Federman can practice his inventiveness. Visual forms are the key.

Visual artists—or poets—or fiction writers—have concerned themselves with patterns of letters and words on paper as one obvious and fairly acceptable means of expression. . . .The experimentation in these areas has shown how inventive artists can be, and how often similar ideas really differ radically from each other.

More and more modern music abolishes itself into silence or discordance fiction poetry write themselves into non-sense or lessnessness.

Aural art involves temporal organization; visual art involves spatial organization. . . .So a poetry, like concrete poetry, that, in our print culture, concentrates on the visual image on the printed page is likely to be concerned substantially with space.

Visual poetry has appeared four times in Occidental art history as an extensive movement—during the Alexandrine period, the Carolingian renaissance, the Baroque & our own day. . . .Each of the past three incarnations appeared at the death of one cultural epoch & the beginning of another.

Offset printing appeals to my more arcane and esoteric tendencies in the same way that other aspects of the process appeal to my need for manual work, my desire for making images, my hopes for craftsmanship, etc. Since early in my experience with offset printing, I've wanted to make works of print art that reflect the process itself.

The notion of "visual poetry" focused anew our interest in traditional forms of singular signs (letters, punctuation marks, elementary symbols, signs for ciphers, etc.) as being "Gestalten" (figures?), in order to interpret them anew and to poetize them freshly, and also—as a forerunner of the so-called written painting!—to demonstrate in many examples the mental-motion process of writing and its realization in the shaping of writing.

Visual poetry is a construction of concrete elements which become expressive in the process of synthesis and arrangement: the FORM of the work is in itself the CONTENT, and whatever expressiveness there is in the work ORIGINATES with the form.

Words and images are used to form a literary polyphony. The verbal narrative forms one line of the polyphony while the drawings, photographs and other visual elements create related yet independent voices throughout the book.

We ask you to accept the edges of the page, as you accept the proscenium which contains the play. Both are places of action, vessels of history, and time passes within at its own measured pace.

That summer of 1969 I discovered. . .that images in sequence could tell a story, whose temporal rhythm is based upon the time a typical reader takes to turn the page.

My aim in working with numbers was no longer the writing of poems and stories but the creation of a numerical field that is both visually and numerally coherent, with varying degrees of visual-numerical complexity.

Although visual literacy may seem an inadequate term to describe the ability to see a picture, it seems not altogether inappropriate when applied to the ability to see/read visual or verbi-visual books. One might also employ the phrase *visual language,* in this connection, to suggest the possibility of sequential development of static visual images (thereby excluding animation, film, television, etc.).

I have tried to help nudge along the idea of book art, whether visual or verbal, or both, over several years, because I was excited by the potential of what I had seen, since it seemed to me, dimly at first, to be the beginning of a recognition that books with visual, or verbi-visual, content could also be profound.

ALL OF THESE PARAGRAPHS ARE DRAWN FROM THE FOLLOWING PAGES.

LITERATURE AND VISION

Aaron Marcus

The earliest of mankind's literatures record a fascination with light in the form of the sun, fire, and the stars. These powerful, mysterious entities were understood as divine phenomena. Directly or indirectly they were apotheosized, thanked, praised, and glorified first in oral, then in written literature. With the development of written languages, the force of light (and indirectly vision) was channeled through a set of carefully nurtured symbol systems. The literature of world civilizations matured as did national tongues and technology. Authors appealed to divine sources for "enlightenment" and passed this understanding on to their communities of readers. Once time and space, action and thought, became captured in writing, literature inevitably became involved with material substances: ink, pen, papyrus, stone, paper, etc. Literature remains a communication of the logical and expressive power of language, but to varying degrees it is also a vehicle for the communication of uniquely visual qualities.

In converting from oral to written forms such as poem, fiction, and essay, "book" literature (to artificially condense history to stereotypical form) restricted the permitted or normative forms. Considering the shades of inflection of the human voice, the written/printed word is a pale transcription of this spectrum. The book as a visual object is at best only a rudimentary visual object. For most of its history in scroll, codex, or book, the visible word has existed like a figure in an ethereal field. For the past several thousand years there has been relatively little tampering with the content or the form of visible language systems, except for a few jarring moments such as that in the ninth century when an official writing system was ordained for Carolingian society or in the fifteenth century when Gutenberg and his followers elaborated upon current and classical letterforms.

If traditional forms of literature can be called verbal literature (whether captured in material such as books or phonograph records), what then constitutes a visual literature? Visual literature exists only in diminutive forms within the strata of book culture. Visual literature occupies a position of some importance in cartography, diagramming, signage, video programming, films, and photography. Many of these forms have certified pedigrees attesting to long use and scholarly interest, others are genuinely modern developments. Visual literature obviously incorporates the use of traditional symbols for visible language, but the important point is this: visual literature begins where language leaves off; it extends mankind's abilities to identify, describe, analyze, evaluate, and extoll the ineffable.

Consider these strange cousins of traditional literature: clearly maps are read as well as seen. They are elementary and direct examples of a visual literature complete with history, popularized forms, academic devotees, and tests for literacy. Diagrams, too, have a similarly long history. They are essentially topological literary forms, often exhibiting no agreed-upon entering point, no method of pronunciation, no sequence of reading, or no exit point. These are qualities which characterize some of the most avant-garde of literary experiments. The use of typography/calligraphy or other non-representational symbols in video and film is less essential, but even "Sesame Street" points to a particular mixture of word and image that more serious *littérateurs* would do well to consider. In photography, the use of printed or written caption/texts together with images constitutes another mixture of the verbal and the non-verbal in a visual form that has considerable merit for literature *quá* visual literature.

Surveying the contemporary forms of poetry, fiction, and essays, one retreats a little surprised and discouraged at the relatively small impact on serious poetry and fiction that twentieth century experimentation in visual literature has had—for example, the impact of concrete poetry from the 1960s and earlier. While literature *quá* visual literature has not progressed significantly, the material of literature has undergone significant change as commerce and technology continued to advance. A selection of contemporary phenomena such as the following indicates some of the developments that are relevant to the future of visual literature:

(1) Advertisements in professional magazines (especially in computer technology) sometimes appear to be striving unselfconsciously for a rare poetic or fictive quality. At times the texts as well as the headlines of these advertisements are written in almost incomprehensible and unpronounceable strings of acronyms that are known only to the respective literati of these professions.

(2) Phonograph album covers achieve the most extravagant and sumptuous visual statements ever created. It is tantalizing to consider what might happen if some political/economic quirk should place the commercial artists responsible for these works in a constructive working association with entrenched *littérateurs*. Were this not to work out, one could turn next to comic book artists.

(3) Houston, Texas, an uncommon city on the frontier of space exploration, boasts superhighways along which are posted colossal electrical, typographic signs with animated messages. These super-signs dwarf the surrounding cityscape and stand like giant captions to the environment.

(4) Many cities have control centers for electricity, traffic, or other complex urban systems in which persons sit completely surrounded by dials, gauges, and graphic displays. Recent research proposals posit such environments as "reading rooms" for future decision makers.

(5) Xerographic posters, reports, photographs, and statements, both in black and white and in color, continue to multiply exponentially. Cable and facsimile/video systems connect businesses in increasing numbers locally, nationally, and internationally. These media create instant literature that reaches audiences without the standard prepackaging of conventional publishing or broadcasting systems.

The antagonism that literature has traditionally shown to technological innovation is well known. That book culture should be conservative is not surprising considering that the first printed books in the fifteenth and sixteenth centuries were held in low esteem by connoisseurs, the typographic innovations of John Baskerville in the eighteenth century were said to induce blindness, and the typewriter-set book is an un-noticed and undeveloped form of the twentieth century. This conservatism is inherent in the means of production and distribution of book culture. In the present century, television and film have begun to supplant the book as a means of cultural literacy, i.e., of binding the culture together. Will conventional literature stand idly by as a passive voyeur of its own *dénouement?* It remains to be seen whether there can be a creative synthesis of the received forms of literature and the emerging systems for communication.

Technological developments will have a profound effect upon the way in which human beings communicate and therefore upon the forms of literature. The most potent of these advances presently reside in laboratories or are limited to use in essentially informational communication systems, rather than aesthetic communication systems. The bright red letters of a digital wristwatch are merely a sign of the times. Other facets of developing technology that will create and influence a visual, *electronic* literature include the following:

(1) Satellite communication systems, including the development of "small dish" antenna systems, will permit individuals to link up directly with satellite relay stations in order to receive and send words and images.

(2) Computer graphics systems of increasing sophistication and in many cases of decreasing cost will permit the processing, translation, and distribution of words and images at great speed. Plasma panels and video projection screens, in particular, will provide computer graphics and video systems with large (e.g., wall-sized) flat displays of alphanumeric symbols or other images. Prices currently run as low as $500.00 for complete computer graphics systems and $1000.00 for complete video recording and playback systems.

(3) Holograms, the special form of displaying light/photographic images in such a way as to produce full three-dimensional color images, can be created via computer graphics systems, can be used in video systems, and can be projected as well as viewed directly. The nature of this communication medium suggests the possibility of three-dimensional texts for a poem, fiction or essay.

(4) Home computers are creating a revolution in the mass use of computers capable of connecting to ubiquitous telephone and television equipment. In particular, facsimile systems, machines for electronically transmitting pictures and writing over long distances, are now being perfected for world-wide use to replace the movement of printed messages and images.

What is the relationship between these technical systems and the future of literature? As often happens, the link between the world of technology/science and arts/humanities is a tenuous one, replete with misunderstanding and misuse of capabilities. Technocrats have little understanding of the implications of their communication systems for humanistic purposes. They often exhibit little interest in the historical, social, and aesthetic impact of their products. Conversely, *littérateurs* have little understanding of the realities, limitations, and potential of emerging communication systems. It must be admitted that they often exhibit a corresponding lack of interest in technical aspects. In this frail link between the Two Cultures lies an unfortunate loss of cross-fertilization. Part of the problem stems from a visual illiteracy on the part of producers as well as the literature-oriented users or potential of emerging systems for visible language display. There is an important lack of symmetry in the situtation. Despite the *littérateur's* ignorance or disdain for modern technology, technology continues its unabated development and conquers new areas of activity and thought.

Printed literature is becoming electronic literature: nonphysical, alphanumeric symbols mixed with other images that are displayed as light. They can be stored, distributed, and enjoyed anywhere at any time. Once again the powerful theme of light and its impact on civilization emerges, perhaps more strongly than ever before. The visual form of literature in the coming decades will be a literature of light. Every facet of technology is leading in this direction: from incorporeal keyboards, to lighted alphanumeric displays, to cathode ray tube and plasma screens. The mystical compulsion which overtakes viewers staring into a television or movie screen is about to be added to the world of the printed word.

The new visual literature will have an unprecedented freedom of kinds of symbols and their placement in space. At last a diagram-like constellation of symbols will become possible, even for the equivalent of "texts" which will give added meaning to the printed, written, photographed, or drawn communication in a two- or even three-dimensional space. This space will be an environmental space that can occupy the entire field of vision and make use of all visual abilities, e.g., depth perception, motion perception, peripheral vision, and color.

A major achievement of electronic communication is the ability to permit rapid two-way communication. This implies a literature that can become active and/or interactive. Once a story teller was a living figure reciting the history of the tribe by firelight. There now exists the possibility of texts moving, appearing and disappearing, responding in controlled or unpredictable ways to the reader/viewer, creating experiences of time that are currently impossible. This dancing array of symbols can be instantly transferred to any point in the world, to any culture.

It is time that the *littérateur* seriously confronted, absorbed, and adapted the changing conditions of communication. The new visual literature will encourage a closer relationship to the direct functioning of the mind and will permit literature to reach audiences currently not accessible. When will "literature" catch up with "vision"? It is hard to predict. The writer/critic George Steiner recently predicted the end of traditional book culture in a new kind of Dark Ages. When will the *littérateur* see the light?

*   *   *

Bibliography

Bolt, Richard A., "Spatial Data Management: Interim Report," Report by the Architecture Machine Group, Massachusetts Institute of Technology, to the Defense Advanced Research Projects Agency, Office of Cybernetics Technology, DARPA Contract No. MDA903-77-C-0037, 1978.

Ewald, William R., Jr., "Information, Perception and Regional Policy," Report prepared for the National Science Foundation, Washington, U.S. Government Printing Office, 1975.

Herdeg, Walter, ed., *Graphis: Diagrams,* Zurich, Graphis Press, 1974.

Gottschall, Edward M., "Vision 77: Communications and Typographics," Report of a conference on state of the art typesetting and communications held at the Rochester Institute of Technology in May 1977, *Upper and Lower Case,* published by the International Typeface Corporation, Vol. 4, No. 2, and No. 3, 1977.

Marcus, Aaron, *Soft Where, Inc.,* West Coast Poetry Review Press, Reno, Nevada, 1975.

————, "At the Edge of Meaning," *Visible Language,* Vol. 11, No. 2, 1977, pp. 4-21, an introduction to a special issue on the future of visible language in an era of electronic communication.

Martin, James, *Future Developments in Telecommunications,* Englewood Cliffs, N.J., Prentice-Hall, 1971.

Panko, Raymond R. and Rosemarie U. Panko, "An Introduction to Computers for Human Communication," *Communication News,* Vol. 14, No. 12, 1977, pp. 32-34.

Robinson, Arthur H. and Barbara Bartz Petchenik, *The Nature of Maps,* Essays toward Understanding Maps and Mapping, Chicago, The University of Chicago Press, 1976.

Steiner, George, "After the Book?", *Visible Language,* Vol. 6, No. 3, 1972, pp. 197-210.

EARLY FRENCH VISUAL POETRY

David W. Seaman

The phenomenon of visual poetry is as old as the art of writing, although literary interest has focussed on it only in the past decade. This recent attention is inspired largely by the creative explosion occurring in countries around the globe, under the heading of Concrete Poetry.

Some fine anthologies display the wide range of concrete and visual poetry: Mary Ellen Solt's elegant volume, *Concrete Poetry: A World View* (Bloomington, 1968), is most comprehensive; other important collections are Emmett Williams' *Anthology of Concrete Poetry* (New York, 1968), Stephan Bann's *Concrete Poetry* (London, 1967), and Eugene Wildman's *Anthology of Concretism* (Chicago, 1967). An extensive historical survey of visual poetry is Massin's *Letter and Image* (New York, 1970); another valuable work is *George Herbert's Pattern Poems: In Their Tradition,* by Dick Higgins (New York, 1977).

To even the casual observer it would be clear that no satisfactory definition could embrace all the forms of visual poetry, variously identified as technopaegnia, pattern-poems, concretism, spatialism, and so forth. Yet what holds true for all of visual poetry is that to achieve its full effect, language *must be visually perceived.*

We associate this quality with the earliest writing by man because it was properly "picture-writing"; the separation of visual image and phonetic symbol that gave us an alphabet was a step taken in a direction away from this aspect of language. But the element of pictorial communication in writing—its semiotic value—has never been entirely forgotten. Plato, for example, suggests in the *Cratylus* that the shape of the letter O is important to the meaning of the word for "round." Another Greek was the creator of the first self-conscious visual poems: Simias of Rhodes (ca. 300 B.C.) wrote three shaped epigrams (called then technopaegnia) that are included in the celebrated *Greek Anthology* (or *Palatine Anthology*). By varying the length of the horizontal lines, Simias formed an axe, a pair of wings, and an egg (which was apparently inscribed on a real egg).

Latin poets also contributed some visual poems of their own. Optatian, a fourth-century successor to Simias, produced an original poem shaped like a hydraulic organ, which actually gives us some rare information about the nature of the instrument. In the Carolingian renaissance around 800 A.D., monastic poets developed the acrostic—already known to the Greeks and Romans—into a complex form of visual poetry. By carefully spacing the letters of each line, and using alternate spellings to make each line equal in length, they

formed a matrix upon which was indicated a super-imposed design,
usually by means of colored letters. The following section of a poem
by Joseph Scott, a disciple of Alcuin, demonstrates the technique.
The bold-face letters are part of the horizontal lines, but make up a
shaped text of their own:

```
.....S A L U S C U N C T I.....
     A Q U A M R E C T O R
     U L G I S U O T O M E
     T A C R U X S A L U E
     S U I T A S A L U S H
     O P T E R C U R R I T
     M E N S P R O P E R A
     I T E T A E T E R N A
     L E S T E D E C U S C
     L U X S A E C L I S S
     E R E U E N E R A N D
     I C O M O T U L E R A
     F E R O C I S P E S L
                 S
```

   The acrostic and its derivations were some of the first visual poetic
forms exploited in the vernacular. Our first poem in this collection is
a multiple acrostic by Eustorg de Beaulieu which partakes of the spirit of the Latin poem above. Beaulieu was a priest and reformed min-
ister, accomplished both as poet and musician. The poem shown here
was on the last page of his *Les Divers Rapportz* (1537), and it can be
read from the capital G in the center, zig-zagging in any manner toward any corner. In theme and form it is a precursor to the work of
Dom Sylvester Houédard, a twentieth-century man of the cloth.
   Francois Villon used acrostics in numerous poems, often signing
his name in this fashion in the *envoi* of a ballad. Some of the most
poignant lines of this student and vagabond are written thus around
his name, as if he desired to attest personally to a certain view of the
medieval world. In the *envoi* to the *Ballade des contre-verités,* included here, he expresses not only the anguish but also the hopes of
his world.
   After Villon we must wait until the seventeenth century to find
more acrostics, mostly anonymous verses by cavaliers and poets of
the court. Many of these are collected in *Le Cabinet Satyrique,* a
volume of satirical poems first published in 1618, and amplified in
1700. Like many poems in this anthology, the one we have chosen
hides a surprise ending and lewd suggestions in the letters of the acrostic. The spirit of preciosity which dominated the behavior of the

salons no doubt affected these verses; one who prefers to call a mirror "le conseiller de la beauté" would also seek to clothe naughty words in an acrostic.

The rebus is a more complex device, demanding that the poem be deciphered as one reads. The rebus was generally based on the placement of the words or parts of words in relation to each other. The adverb describing the relationship then became part of the poem. For example, $^{sta}_{we}{}^{nd}$ is read "we *under*stand." In another type of rebus, numerals and letters are used for their homonyms, as in the English T-4-2, "tea for two." Isidore Isou and members of the modern Lettrist movement rely heavily on the rebus, and contend that it is an advanced form of communication. In the Renaissance, this type of poetry was practiced by the so-called Grands Rhétoriqueurs, who indulged in all sorts of intricate metrical, visual, and rhyming devices. The first poem we present in this category is by Jean Marot, father·of Clément and a courtier under Anne de Bretagne and François 1er This is a *rondeau* using a rebus in every line. As an additional aid to our readers, the deciphered French is offered before the translation, with the adverbs italicized. In the French of Marot's time, "over" is expressed by *sur* and *su* (also spelled *ceu*), and "under" is expressed by *sous* and *sub;* the reader should also watch for *entre.*

The following poem uses the other class of rebuses, requiring the oral reading of written letters. This points up the difference between the actual signs used in writing and the name we give them; often, the function in writing has nothing to do with the appellation. Thus when the poem is read aloud it sounds normal, but the visual notation is full of surprises. This particular poem is recorded by Estienne Tabourot in his collection of literary curiosities called *Les Bigarrures* (1616). He explains that it is the school report given by a headmistress to the mother of a girl student. The original text ostensibly tells about her writing lessons, but the deciphered version, as offered by Tabourot, describes her behavior, and even this holds a double meaning. Modern readers must bear in mind that at the time of composition *M* was pronounced *ame,* and that *V* was interchanged with *U.*

Creative jongleurs of the late Middle Ages and the Renaissance also liked the *vers batelés,* or juggled verses. This practice consisted of writing lines which could be read in more than one direction. The fifteenth-century courtier Jean Meschinot wrote a hymn to the Virgin which he claimed could be read in thirty-two different fashions. In the first of our two selections of *vers batelés,* Jean Bouchet writes about going to law court. His final couplet reveals the trick: by reading straight across the lines one finds a certain meaning, but reading down the two columns one receives the opposite message.

The second juggled poem here is also about law, and we might well observe that these ambiguous verses reflect a then prevalent critical attitude toward members of the bar. Jean Bouchet was a magistrate of the early Renaissance and thus probably speaks from experience when he equivocates on the qualities of lawyers: read to the right, he declares, and lawyers are good, but if you read backwards it turns out they are sly.

In spite of the wit of some other forms, the most approachable early visual poems are the *technopaegnia.* The Greek origins were still evident in the work of Melin de Sainct-Gelays, a sixteenth-century courtier. His wings are the bearers of the news that occasioned his exaggerated rejoicing: the mother of the King, known as Madame, though fatally ill, made an apparent recovery. The archaic spelling of *ailes* (wings) also hints at the meaning *à elle* (to her).

By the sixteenth century and the time of the Renaissance in England, writing shaped verse became a literary nicety, and George Puttenham obliged with instructions on how to do it in his *Arte of English Poesie* (1589). Puttenham had knowledge of the Greek egg-shaped poem, but he claimed that his main source was Oriental poetry. It is certainly true that some poems in Arabic calligraphy were written in extraordinary shapes, and Puttenham may have seen some of them. In any case, he gives the metrical schemes for forming a variety of geometric shapes, and even suggests a symbolic value to some of them. (The taper, for example, signifies hope, and thus should be used in exchanging love letters.) While Puttenham's influence is disputed, his concern for shaped visual poetry certainly reflected an interest of his contemporaries. A prolific composer of these forms was Richard Willes, whose *Poematum liber* (1573) contains concrete poems in the shape of pyramids, wings, an altar and a sword. The best-known English poet to follow this tradition is George Herbert, in the seventeenth century. His metaphysical poems in *The Temple* include an *Altar* and *Easter Wings.*

The French have preferred representational shapes of a more common status: glasses and bottles are the favorite subjects. François Rabelais uses a bottle-shaped poem in the Fifth Book of *Gargantua et Pantagruel.* The hero Panurge is led to the oracle of *la Dive Bouteille,* the Holy Bottle, where he sings an epileny (harvest song) written in the shape of a bottle. Appropriately, the word of the oracle will be "trinc!"

The rationalists of eighteenth century France rejected visual poetry as frivolous, but the epicureans were host to more goblets and flasks. Charles François Pannard wrote many vaudevilles for the Opéra-comique, and composed numerous drinking songs. Although songs normally lose their charm when written down, the two we present here reveal their full magic only when seen in printed form; they are among the most elegant examples of early French visual poetry.

They match the concrete form to the subject, and they create the form according to the metrical principles Puttenham insisted on. It is not a matter of extending or compressing lines of type to make a shape, but rather of causing the shape to proceed naturally from the length of the lines. In the case of the goblet shown here, the shortness of the monosyllabic lines also concurs with the urgency reported by the thirsty poet.

We conclude our descriptions with a lute by Robert Angot. This poem is part of the "Concert des muses françoises" in his *Chef d'Oeuvre poétique* (1634). We notice at once a technique that distinguishes Angot from the other poets whose work is gathered here: Angot demonstrates an early attempt to break down this straight linear matrix of the printed page. Three of his five visual poems use such devices as turning the print sideways or obliquely, curving lines of print, and adding hand-drawn designs. In our lute, the sound box is outlined with a curving line of type which can be written as a regular octosyllabic quatrain. The opening in the sound box is a circular emblem with a Latin motto, and there is also a Latin motto at the top of the fingerboard. The main part of the poem, making up the eight strings of the instrument, runs vertically on the page, which must be turned on its left side. The reader is thus obliged to become physically engaged in the act of reading the poem. With the addition of some sketched-in tuning keys, this instrument is clearly and simply depicted. While hardly a modern concrete poem, this lute displays an amazing appreciation of print as a concrete means of expression, and equals in suppleness the mandoline created by Apollinaire.

The contemporary movement in visual poetry is not an isolated phenomenon. While its immediate sources are in Mallarmé's *Un Coup de dés* and the efforts of Futurism, Dadaism, and Surrealism, it benefits also from a long tradition of verbal experimentation that has manifested itself in every period of French literature.

Eustorg de Beaulieu (1495? -- 1552)

Gloire à Dieu seul	Glory to God Alone
luesueidieuseul	enoladoGodalone
uesueidadieuseu	noladoGogodalon
esueidaeadieuse	oladoGotoGodalo
sueidaereadieus	ladoGotytoGodal
ueidaerireadieu	adoGotyrytoGoda
eidaerioireadie	doGotyrorytoGod
idaerioloireadi	oGotyrolorytoGo
daeriolGloiread	GotyrolGlorytoG
idaerioloireadi	oGotyrolorytoGo
eidaerioireadie	doGotyrorytoGod
ueidaerireadieu	adoGotyrytoGoda
sueidaereadieus	lodoGotytoGodal
esueidaeadieuse	oladoGotoGodalo
uésueidadieuseu	noladoGoGodalon
luesueidieuseul	enoladoGodalone

Francois Villon (1431 - 1463?)

Envoi de la Ballade des contre-vérités

Voulez vous que vérité die:
Il n'est jouer qu'en maladie,
Lettre vraye que tragedie,
Lasche homme que chevaleresque,
Orrible son que melodie,
Ne bon conseil que d'amoureux.

Envoi to the Ballad of the Counter-Truths

Do you want the truth from me?
Well, there is no joy save in sickness,
No truer words than in tragedies,
No cowards other than knights,
No horrid sounds except in songs,
Nor better advice than from lovers.

Anonymous (c. 1700)

Filles qui languissez dans les pâles couleurs,
Obéissez au Dieu qui règne sur les coeurs.
Vous souffrez chaque jour des peines infernales;
Tout ce mal ne provient que d'extremes chaleurs.
Eprouvez ce secret pour guérir vos douleurs:
Suivez de ces six vers les lettres capitales.

Girls who, pale of color, languish,
Obey the God who reigns over the heart.
For days you suffer infernal anguish;
Undue heat is the only cause of this hurt.
Come try this secret to cure your pains:
Keep to the capitals of these six lines.

Jean Marot (1450? - 1526)

L'Homme dupé

riant   fuz   nagueres
  En   pris

to-D'une-us   affectée.

espoir   haitée
  Que   vent
         j'ay

Mais   d   quand pr-s'amour-is
      fuz

                   ris
Car   j'apper   ses mignards
      que

  traicts
Estoient   d'amour mal a
                      e e

riant
  En

l'oeil
Escus   de   elle a pris
      moy

maniere ruzée
te-me-nant

Et quand je veux e-faire-e
        elle

Me dit que mal apris
      to-y-us

riant.
  En

En *sous*riant fuz nagueres *sur*pris
D'une *sub*tile *entre* tous affectée,
Que *sous* espoir j'ay *sou*vent *sous*haitée;
Mais de*ceu* fuz quand s'amour *entre*pris,
Car j'apper*ceu* que ses mignards *sous*ris
Estoient *sous*traicts d'amour mal as*sur*ée,
En *sous*riant.

Escus *sous* l'oeil, *sous* de moy elle a pris,
M'*entre*tenant *sous* maniere ruzée;
Et quand je veux *sur* elle faire *entr*ée,
Me dit que *su*is *entre* tous mal appris
En *sous*riant.

Duped

While smiling, I was recently surprised
By a subtle girl, putting on airs in the crowd,
Such as I have always wishfully desired.
But I was deceived when I undertook her suit,
For I perceived that her sugary smiles
Were the devices of an unreliable love
By smiling.

Her eye on money, she took my pennies,
Entertaining me in a cunning way;
And when I want to make overtures to her,
I'm rather ill-informed, she tells me
Smiling.

Anonymous (c. 1600)

Vostre fillette en ses escrits
Recherche trop ses a a.
L met trop d'ancre en son I,
L s trop ses V V ouverts,
Puis son K tourne de travers
Et couche trop le Q infame;
C'est cela qui gaste son M.

Vostre fillette en ses escrits
Recherche trop ses appetits.
Elle met trop d'ancre en son nid,
Et laisse trop ses huis ouverts.
Puis son cas tourne de travers,
Et couche trop le cu infame;
C'est cela qui gaste son ame.

Your little girl, in her writing lessons,
Works too much on her small a's.
She puts too much ink in her I,
And she leaves her U's too open.
Then she turns her K askew
And lays out a messy Q;
That's what is ruining her M.

Your little girl, in what she writes,
Seeks out too much her appetites.
She puts too much anchor into her nest,
And too often leaves her windows agape.
She isn't straightforward, for the rest,
And she sleeps too often with her bottom foul;
That is what is spoiling her soul.

Jean Bouchet (1476 - 1557?)

Heureux est il   Celui qui n'a procès
Qui plaidera   N'est prins pour homme sage;
S'il est subtil   On lui faict des excès;
Mal il n'aura   S'il n'est rempli d'oultrage.
          Allez droict, vous ne plaiderez;
          Sincopez: procès vous aurez.

Happy is he   He who has no case
Whoever will sue   Isn't taken for a sage;
If subtle he'll be   He's heaped with excess;
He'll have no rue   If he's not full of outrage.
          Go straight, you won't sue;
          But divide, and you do.

Lisez au droict, verrez les tours
Des bons, des mauvais au rebours.

Practiciens, sont bons, non feincts,
Gracieux, non mal desirans,
Rien refusans, non inhumains,
Conscientieux, non tirans.

Read to the right, you'll see the traits
of the good; of the bad if you read in reverse.

Lawyers are good, not sly,
Gracious, not wishing ill,
Anything refusing, not inhuman,
Conscientious, not tyrannical.

Melin de Sainct-Gelays (1491 - 1558)

A la Guerison de Madame, Mère de François 1er

O heureuse nouvelle, ò desireux rapport
  De la santé de qui la maladie
    Estoit fin de plus d'une vie!
      O aggreable port,
        Dont les plaisirs
          Sont égaux
            Aux travaux!
          Des longs desirs,
        O favorable sort!
      Et toy, ò mon ame assouvie,
    Qu'attends-tu plus? as-tu encore envie
D'avoir un plus grand bien ça bas avant la Mort?

Oh happy news, oh desirous report
  On the health of her whose malady
    Was the end of more lives than one!
      Oh pleasant burden
        Whose pleasures
          Are equal
            To the labor!
        After long wishing,
      What a favorable outcome!
    And you, Oh my assuaged soul,
  What more do you wait? do you still wish
To have a greater gift in this world before your Death?

François Rabelais (1494? - 1553)

O
Bouteille
Pleine toute
De mistères,
D'une oreille
Je t'escoute:
Ne différez
Et le mot proférez
Auquel pend mon cueur!
En la tant divine licqueur,
Qui est dedans tes flans reclose,
Bachus, que fut d'Inde vaincqueur,
Tient toute vérité enclose.
Vin tant divin, loing de toy est forclose
Toute mensonge et toute tromperye,
En joye soit l'âme de Noé close,
Lequel de toy nous fit la tempérye.
Sonne le beau mot je t'en prye,
Qui me doibt oster de misère.
Ainsi ne se perde une goutte
De toy, soit blanche, ou soit vermeille,
O Bouteille
Pleine toute
De mistères!

O
Bottle
All full
Of mysteries
With one ear
I listen;
Do not wait,
Give me the word
On which my heart hangs!
In the liquor so divine
Which is enclosed within your sides,
Bacchus, who was conqueror of India
Keeps all truths enclosed.
Wine so divine, far from you is foreclosed
All lying and all deceit;
Let Noah's soul rest in joy,
He who made you our fair weather.
Sound the beautiful word, I pray,
Which must raise me out of misery.
Therefore let no drop be lost
From you, either white or red,
O Bottle
All full
Of mysteries.

Charles François Pannard (1694? - 1765)

Nothing can we find upon the Earth
So good or so lovely as a glass.
Charming cradle of tender love,
It's you, country fern,
It's you who serve to make
The happy instrument
Where often fizzes,
Foams and sparkles
The juice that makes us
Gay, laughing,
Content.
What sweetness
It brings to the heart!
Soon,
Soon,
Soon,
Bring me some,
Ring it out,
Now,
Now,
Now,
Give me some,
Fast and just right.
One can see in its darling floods
Gaiety and Laughter brimming.

Nous ne pouvons rien trouver sur la terre,
Quit soit si bon, ni si beau que le verre.
Du tendre amour berceau charmant,
C'est toi, champêtre fougere
C'est toi, qui sers à faire
L'heureux instrument
Où souvent pétille,
Mousse et brille
Le jus qui rend
Gai, riant,
Content.
Quelle douceur
Il porte au coeur!
Tôt,
Tôt,
Tôt,
Qu' on m'en donne,
Qu' on l'entonne.
Tôt,
Tôt,
Tôt,
Qu'on m'en donne
Vite et comme il faut.
L'on y voit, sur ses flots chéris,
Nager l'Allegresse et le Ris.

Que mon
Flacon
Me semble bon!
Sans lui,
L'ennui
Me nuit,
Me suit;
Je sens
Mes sens
Mourans,
Pensans.
Quand je le tien,
Dieux! que je suis bien!
Que son aspect est agréable!
Que je fais cas de ses divins présens!
C'est de son sein fécond, c'est de ses heureux flancs
Que coule ce nectar si doux, si délectable,
Qui rend tous les esprits, tous les coeurs satisfaits.
Cher objet de mes voeux, tu fais toute ma gloire.
Tant que mon coeur vivra, de tes charmants bienfaits
Il scaura conserver la fidelle mémoire.
Ma Muse, à te louer, se consacre à jamais.
Tantôt dans un cave, tantôt sous une treille,
Ma lyre, de ma voix accompagnant le son,
Répetera cent fois cette aimable chanson:
Regne sans fin, ma charmante bouteille;
Regne sans cesse mon cher flacon.

Model
Bottle,
Her I'll coddle!
Forlorn,
I'm bored,
Followed
And gored.
Feelings,
Reeling,
Feel like
Dying.
But to hold her,
God! how I smolder!
How her look is agreeable!
How estimable her presence divine!
It's from her fertile breast, it's from her happy side,
That flows this nectar, so sweet, so delectable,
Which renders all men's hearts and their minds satisfied.
Dear object of desire, you make all my glory,
So long as my heart lives, of your charms bona fide
He will know to preserve a faithful memory.
My Muse lives to have you forever glorified.
Whether down in a cellar, or under the stars,
The sound of my lyre, as my voice joins the task,
Will repeat the song where a hundred times we ask:
Reign without cease my bottle and my cask,
Reign without end, my charming flask.

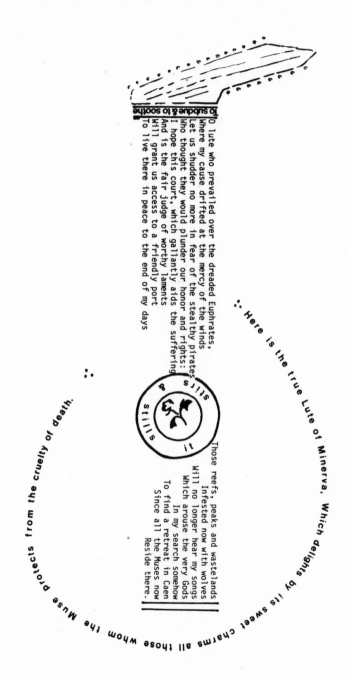

To subdue & to soothe

O lute who prevailed over the dreaded Euphrates,
Where my cause drifted at the mercy of the winds
Let us shudder no more in fear of the stealthy pirates
Who thought they would plunder our honor and rights:
I hope this court, which gallantly aids the suffering
And is the fair judge of worthy laments
Will grant us access to a friendly port
To live there in peace to the end of my days

stirs & stills it

Here is the true Lute of Minerva, Which delights by its sweet charms all those whom the Muse protects from the cruelty of death.

Those reefs, peaks and wastelands
Infested now with wolves
Will no longer hear my songs
Which arouse the very Gods
In my search somehow
To find a retreat in Caen
Since all the Muses now
Reside there.

ON THE NEED FOR A VISUAL LITERATURE — WHAT THE "LITERATURE" OFFERS

There is a growing awareness today of the importance of visual imagery as an embodiment of thought. Nowhere is this more evident than in medieval studies. ...In some respects the impact made across the centuries by shapes, patterns, and images is more direct than that of words.
—Marjorie Reeves & Beatrice Hirsch-Reich, *The* Figurae *of Joachin of Fiore* (Oxford University Press, 1972).

I suppose we can always describe what we've seen more effectively than what we've heard.
—Gilles Atter in More's *Utopia.*

The most highly relationed feelings are the visual, and these are of all the feelings the most easily reproduced in thought.
—Herbert Spencer, *Psychology.*

So great is the average mathematician's distrust of purely verbal arguments that Hilbert beginning about 1925 proposed that mathematicians forget about the "meanings" of their elaborate game with symbols and concentrate on the game itself.
—E.T. Bell, *The Queen of the Sciences* (1931).

The world of words has shrunk....the word, especially in its sequential, typographic forms, may have been an imperfect, perhaps transitory code.
—George Steiner, *Language and Silence.*

We make for ourselves pictures of facts.
                            —Wittgenstein.

The word is not dead; it is changing its skin.
                            —Dick Higgins.

Verbivocalvisual.   —James Joyce (& H.M. McLuhan).

Though the text of scientific publications is mostly beyond my means of comprehension, the figures with which they are illustrated bring me occasionally on the track of new possibilities for my work. It was thus that a fruitful conctact could be made between mathematicians and myself.
—M.C. Escher, in C.H. Macgillavry, *Symmetry Aspects of M.C. Escher's Drawings* (Utrecht, 1965).

Magritte's lovely page on words and images.

Pictures speak louder than words. One picture is worth a thousand words.
—Proverbs (it all depends!).

Discard words for a moment and contemplate facts more directly than images. . . .The highest philosophical capacity requires a combination of vision with abstract words.
—Bertrand Russell, *The Analysis of Mind.*

In any case, to me, all script is visual, because letters have shapes that are audiovisual pictures of the speech organs making sound. (Hegel, Spinoza, Voltaire as authorities). So all *lite*rature is to that extent visual anyway.

— Peter Mayer

THE STRATEGY OF VISUAL POETRY: THREE ASPECTS

Dick Higgins

As soon as the visual aspect of a poem becomes not just incidental but is actually structural, the strategy of a poem is affected in several ways: (1) the momentum of a linear thrust is broken, since the eye must stop and take note of the shape. A static element is thereby introduced. (2) The idea of the work is less exclusively dependent upon the words of the text and can even become somewhat transcendent to the verbal text. (3) In the case of visual poems which are primarily visual and only lesserly textural—the verbally poetic visual piece—a similar metamorphosis occurs: the verbal aspect becomes transcendent to its visual embodiment, and a kinetic thrust becomes possible in a way that very few visual art works can have. To make a few beginnings and substantiations of these observations is the purpose of this paper.

1-The Breaking of the Linear Thrust

Among the traditional thoughts of a poem which a poet tends to keep as a paradigm in his mind is the idea of the poem that "catches you up, and won't let go of you until you have finished reading the poem." In our western culture this is almost the normative view. It is the source of "power" in a poem. There is an element of compulsion which leads ultimately to catharsis, the touchstone criterion which Aristotle attributed to the tragedies of Sophocles. But Aristotle belonged to a time in Greek culture when it was no longer possible to rest content with the earlier civic virtues and the mental and poetic culture of the previous generation. Greek civilization was becoming obliged to conquer or to be conquered: and the linear philosophy which he developed was geared towards proof and demonstration, ultimately towards power. The aim of his rhetoric is to persuade. The goal of our rhetoric today is far less to persuade than to develop the mental or perceptual resource, to share the experience. Applied to rhetoric, this means that our goal is less to persuade (at least by logical means) than to show in such a way what it feels like to think this or that, what happens if one does think this or that way, and to clothe the thought, therefore, *in the most vivid and memorable embodiment possible* rather than the most logically defensible one. The linear expression of an Aristotelian logic is apt to be left to lawyers: the artists have other concerns.

But the normative taste has been, in poetry, for the powerful poem. The poems that reject this have been damned as decadent, feeble or impotent. Even our occidental lyricism has been power-oriented. As I've noted elsewhere, Shelley's "Ode to a Skylark" seems

to be more about a fighter plane than about a bird. Yet each generation must reinvent its arts in its own image; that is the inner drive towards realism, and to go against it can only lead to an art of shallow
and hollow gesture. As power is removed from our options, it can be
replaced with new criteria that were always there but were undervalued—truth, serenity, harmony. The work which is *forced* to be only
one thing, because serious works are thought to be only one thing,
may be logically defensible, but it will tend to be experientially inadequate. Thus the drive to make works which are conceptually intermedial—whose essence lies between the traditional media—gathers
momentum today as part of a great variety of what passes for "movements" on our cultural scene, though without being a movement in
its own right. Many times in history intermedia have appeared—in
India following the Hindu revival (and again following the Moslem
conquest), in Italy at the end of the renaissance—[1] and in many other
times and places as well. But we see some Italian instances of this
drive towards intermedia in the literary and emblematic painting of
the late sixteenth century, the many pattern poems of the period
(of which more presently), in the emblematic imagery of such works
as Giordano Bruno's *Degli Eroici Furori* and in his almost semiotic
ideas of syncretic imagery in such later Latin writings as his *De Imag-
inum, Signorum et Idearum Compositione* ("On the Composition of
Images, Signs and Ideas") of 1591,[2] and even in the appearance of
the opera, which is, however, more of a mixed medium than an intermedium, since there is no conceptual fusion between text, music and
mise-en-scène; the components of a mixed medium remain separate
though simultaneous. However, the syncretism of the following quotation from Bruno could equally well serve to describe the theoretical
underpinnings of many artists' work since the late 1950's:[3]

> Therefore, and in a certain measure, philosophers are painters; poets
> are painters and philosophers; painters are philosophers and poets. He who
> is not a poet and a painter is no philosopher. We say rightly that to under-
> stand is to see imaginary forms and figures; and understanding is fancy, at
> least it is not deprived of fancy. He is no painter who is not in some degree
> a poet and thinker, and there can be no poet without a certain measure of
> thought and representation.

Thus, returning to the visual poetry of today, it is easy for us to see
how the syncretism of a Bruno fits well with the formal syncretism
of recent visual poetry and parallel art forms—conceptual art, Fluxus
performances and Happenings, for instance—and indicates the synchronic appropriateness of it, given our cultural milieu. Of course the
pattern poem of the past tended to be strongly mimetic—to take the
shape of a natural object rather than a geometrical or other schematic form. Here for instance is a very typical pattern poem of this sort:

Fig. 1—Bonifacio Baldessare, from *Musarum Libri* (1628). This heart-shaped poem has a text which falls quite naturally into its shape: many similar pieces do not, but rather the text seems forced into a visual form, like a Procrustean bed. But many traditional poems, too, seem forced to *remain* non-visual when the natural thing for them would be to take shape and fly, if only they were to follow their own inner logic.

Of the roughly 1100 pattern poems that I have collected from before 1900, probably 85 percent are representational in the sense of the above example, and only about 15 percent are as schematic as the one given below, as an example of the other type:

Fig. 2—Amaracandra Sūri, from the *Kāvyakalpalatā* (ca. 1297 A.D.). The Latin Middle Ages abound with cabalistic arrays of letters into grids, moving metatactically from magic into art, whose "inscriptions" can also be rearranged readily into traditional poetry. Several examples will be found in my book on pattern poems, cited in the footnotes. But just to show how universal this phenomenon is, here is an example in Gujarati, an Indian language from the area north of Bombay. This is one of many examples collected by Prof. Hiralal R. Kapadia and printed in various issues of the *Journal of the University of Bombay* in 1954 and 1955 and elsewhere. Prof. Kapadia gives written-out versions for this text and others, which would otherwise appear to be simply diagrams.

अष्टार-चक्र (68-69)

Modern visual poetry tends, however, to be far less mimetic. The visual element is often purely expressive and improvised, in the manner of an abstract expressionist painting. Or it is clean and geometrical. Or its forms are not those of natural objects, but of the ways and processes of nature. Thus the familiar Apollinaire rain calligramme shows the words scattered down the page as rain falls, and not spread out into a lattice on the page, as if the falling raindrops could be photographed with a time-stop mechanism. The array of words may be schematic or linguistic; it may resemble the flowcharts of a computer programmer's diagram. But what it always does is follow some sort of spatialized method which requires, for the fullest enjoyment of the piece, that we become sensitized to the spatial aspect of the piece. The space is not just a notation, at best a stand-in for time, as is the tendency in traditional poetry. Rather, it is a structural unit which may serve a large variety of purposes.

2-The Poem Transcends the Verbal Text

Perhaps at this point the concept of metataxis should be introduced. This is a term used in anthropology to describe the shift in function (which determines a shift in identity) of an object from one situation to another. A horse, once a means of transportation, becomes a symbol of status or leisure. A bow and arrow, formerly an instrument of war or a hunting tool, is metatactically altered into being a child's toy. Elsewhere I have pointed out how magical and cabalistic devices, originally intended as metaphors for a hidden truth, became instead metaphors for an aesthetic truth; this explains the art forms of some of the earlier pattern poems.[4] A similar process seems to be involved, as one looks at the role of text in the concrete poems of the 1960's and before, and as one compares them with the *poesia visiva* works of the 1970's. These former usually consisted of arrays of letters or words, while the latter are for more visual than verbal or textual: many consist of photographs of people carrying words or even letters, others show something happening to the words or letters—a process of erasure, metamorphosis, dissolution or reconstruction.

For anyone who has followed visual poetry or concrete poetry for any length of time, this distinction which I am making between the more text- or letter-oriented sort and the more purely visual variety will come as no surprise. Most of the works in the two major anthologies of the 1960's, those edited by Emmett Williams (*An Anthology of Concrete Poetry*, 1967) and by Mary Ellen Solt (*Concrete Poetry: A World View*, 1968) are of the first sort, while those in more recent books, such as those edited by Jean-François Bory (*Once Again*, 1968) and by Klaus Peter Dencker (*Text-Bilder: Visuelle Poesie International*, 1972) include many examples of the latter. A number of the informal magazines devoted to the most visual sort of work have come out of Italy, and so this sort has come to be known by an Italian term for "visual poetry," "poesia visiva." Some writers such as Klaus Peter Dencker have tried to make a qualitative distinction and a hard line between concrete poetry and "visual poetry" (by which he means *poesia visiva*) and Dencker is currently at work on a large anthology of *poesia visiva* through the centuries—sculptural poems and object poems from the past, up to the most current sort of photographic poems. A hard-line qualitative distinction is, in my opinion, not possible, but a general quantitative one, based on the degree within the intermedial polarity between text- or visual-orientation, is useful for taxonomic purposes. Anyone who wants to distinguish and verbalize the differences between the concrete or verbal sort, as in the works of Eugen Gomringer, Mary Ellen Solt, the earlier Ian Hamilton Finlay or Jonathan Williams, and the new works by Finlay (the sailboats), Alain Arias-Misson or Thomas Ockerse, will find this distinction useful. For those photographic sequence-works of *poesia visiva* that are extremely close to some works of concept art, such as some pieces by Robert Smithson, it is almost impossible to get a sense of text when one reads the work. In a piece by Jean-François Bory, one sees photographs of a book left on the sand, the tide comes in and bears it away—and it sinks. There may have been words in the book. But does it matter what these were? The criteria for evaluating the nature and impact of such a work are those which would be used for photo-journalism or for a performance—in fact, such a work tends to feel like the documentation of a performance which one is to imagine, but which may or may not have taken place. Not only the grammar of the text is gone, but the words as well. Because there is so much of this *poesia visiva* being done right now, one is apt to forget that it has been done for a long time. It is nearly twenty years since Emmett Williams's "Poetry Clock" (1959) was made; it appeared in his anthology. And, in a sense and to a degree, many of the geometric paintings of the Swiss school of the post-war years, which are historically ancestral to the term "concrete poetry," can be regarded as wordless poems. I mean of course paintings by Richard Löhse, the early Karl Gerstner, and Max Bill, the last of whom called many of his works which appeared to be physical realizations (concretizations?) of an intellectual principle or progression "Konkretionen," which we would translate as "concretions." His secretary in the early 1950's was Eugen Gomringer, to whom the term "concrete poetry" is usually attributed, and who used the term by analogy to Bill's works. Many works by Bill and Löhse and others of that group consist of series and progressions and even permutations, and the progressions of shapes or colors are analogous to the behavior of verbal elements in what are sometimes referred to as "Proteus poems" after a famous poem by Julius Caesar Scaliger. In the paint-

ings, the progression is one of verbal units. Here are two examples,
the first from Scaliger's "Proteus" (ca. 1561):[6]

> Perfide sperasti divos te fallere Proteu
> Perfide te divos sperasti fallere Proteu
> Perfide te sperasti divos fallere Proteu
> Perfide te Proteu sperasti fallere divos
> Perfide sperasti te divos fallere Proteu
> . . .

And here is a brief passage from Jackson Mac Low's "JAIL BREAK
(for Emmett Williams & John Cage) September 1963. April & August
1966:"[7]

> Tear now jails down all.
> Tear all now down jails.
> Tear now all jails down.
> Tear jails now all down.
> Tear jails now down all.
> . . .

The relation of such "Proteus poems" to concrete poetry is that what
syntax there is is geometric rather than, as in traditional poetry, alge-
braic—cumulative rather than linear. The elements taken separately
have no particular power or impact. But each line gets nearly all its
meaning from its relation to the others, where in traditional poetry
the lines normally make some sense even when isolated. In a geometric painting, shapes get their relevance from their relation to other
shapes, and in a "Proteus poem" the pattern of the components is far
more important than just what they happen to be.

In fact, in many cases the pattern is made clearer and more vivid by
using elements that relate to words but are not words—numbers, the
letters of the alphabet, or visual vocabularies. I made a series of one-
of-a-kind (mostly) silk-screen prints using a vocabulary of 300 elements, repeated and juxtaposed in a variety of ways to make almost
900 different works. There is no need for the viewer to see all the
works in this series, which is called *7.7.73*; there is just enough information to establish the pattern in a clear and indelible way. Each
work in the series is analogous to a line in a poem—and in a "Proteus
poem" there is seldom a need to go through every possible line, every
possible permutation. The lines of such a work tend to be synecdoc-
hal—the parts of the work can stand for the whole. Many of Emmett
Williams's pieces in his *Anthology of Concrete Poetry* will serve as
examples of the alphabet poem genre, and the number poems of
Richard Kostelanetz or Ladislav Nebesky can illustrate this latter category. Some works of visual art are analogous to these poems—especially certain paintings by Jasper Johns and Robert Indiana. But
these latter seem, for the most part, geared to a luxury market and

not to the page or the poor connoisseur's library: for social reasons, one would tend, then, to class these last as paintings more than as poems.

3—The Transcendent Text

In the works which I have discussed up to now, the effect has been seen of the introduction of spatial considerations and visual elements into verbal materials, progressively, until their structure is no longer dependent upon any verbal text, though something of a verbal method of experiencing the work remains—the process of reading, of abstracting a sort of verbal pattern from the work and subsumption of the visual dimension into that verbal framework. But of course the opposite is true too—that there can be visual works whose impact depends upon their association with the word, the logos. This is true of many religious works. There can be a metataxis from a religious or mystical perception into a political one, as in the case of the highly emblematic iconography of many works from the period of the French Revolution and the Napoleonic Era. Or there can be (and this is what concerns us more here) an emblematic array of images which embody a verbal message. In its extreme, this could be the rebus, taken as an art form (as it was, for instance, by the French Renaissance poet Clement Marot). Or it could be simply the emblem literature of the late Renaissance and Baroque, the emblem books of Francis Quarles and others, or even the works of William Blake, such as *The Marriage of Heaven and Hell.* For these, the grammar and pattern of literature are not superimposed over the visual art base, necessarily, but rather the verbal image and often the word itself is included. This would be the case with a good many advertising illustrations, obviously. But it is also the area, conceptually, of the calligraphic text, the "drawing of words." This has not been a very productive area for avant-garde visual poetry, just now. The highest products of this have been the calligraphic poems of Paul Reps, or the various collaborations between abstract expressionist painters and poets in the 1960's, between Larry Rivers and Frank O'Hara, for instance. In such work, one tends to abstract from the whole not so much a reading as a number of discrete words or images, to notice the pattern and then let the work go as a whole. Put linguistically, one sees the *langue* incompletely because one is not caught up by the component *paroles.*

Yet, to put the question philosophically, could there not be a work of this sort which was independent of the words which comprised it? A work of pure form, a matrix into which anything which was put comprised the realization of the work? This is a question which any translator must face: but often it is faced, now, by the artist or poet or concrete poet. How can I "translate" my work from text into music? From one realization of a work into another? In such pieces as

The Twin Plays (1963) Jackson Mac Low used an identical matrix of action, sentence structure and so on, to make two different stage works; one set of verbal events was made from all the sounds and syllables in the proper name "Port-au-Prince" and the other came from a list of sayings and proverbs recorded in Adams County, Illinois. A similar assumption is at work in Stephen McCaffery's "homolinguistic translations"—systematic puns from given texts to new ones. The potential here for visual poetry is equally great. It seems likely that blank works will come to exist, which one fills with words, and that these will be a new category in visual poetry. Prototypes have been made already by myself and others. Novels which come on cards which one is expected to shuffle and then read aloud (often with materials which the reader also contributes) have some of this character. But as a genre, the area is yet unexplored.

4-Conclusion

Just as one might imagine from the quotation I gave from Giordano Bruno, there are analogous interfaces and intermedia that are similar to the visual poem in poetry/music (sound poetry), poetry/philosophy (concept poetry), even poetry/technology (what Bern Porter calls "sci-art" poems). These too are very much in need of classification, with an accepted taxonomy. It is very difficult to enjoy a work fully before one has made some mental classification of it, and yet the hermeneutics of such classification are very difficult owing to the lack of any consensus. But without the classification, one is ill-at-ease with a work, unable to relax and live with it. Thus the real need, in understanding visual poetry right now, is not for a dualism of good and bad or true and false, but for an overall teleology of the work which can serve as the basis for both a taxonomy and hermeneutic. For instance, in this paper we have dealt a little with the teleology of visual poetry. But what does this imply for sound poetry? Many sound poems are being distributed on tape cassettes; but one plays a cassette more than once, usually, in a great variety of situations. One hears the cassette at home, and one plays it in one's automobile when one is driving: how does this affect the poem? And in any case, while a traditional poem was made to be witnessed from beginning to end in a book—and was usually designed for its maximum impact to be on first reading (which later readings re-evoke), what is the effect of a sound poem in which one assumes the cassette will be played over and over and over again? The text must be designed for re-experiencing. It must "wear well." Similarly, few traditional poems were designed for putting on one's wall and for living with. Yet many visual poems are designed for just that purpose. How does this affect their nature?

These are questions which have not yet been answered in any satisfactory way, so far as I know.

But to sum up: the potential for visual poetry lies in its introduction of space and visual shape—at the cost of momentum and kinetic inertia. A visual poem, if it has power, will not gain it from the sequence of verbal images in the same way that Vergil's *Aeneid* did, but rather in the way that the powerful anti-Hitler graphic photomontages of John Heartfield do. And in any case, the medium seems more suitable for the achievement of lyrical and analytical effects than for the mighty impact that western poetry sought for during the imperial era. We need not be like Joseph Addison, the Aristotelian critic in the 18th century, who, in the *Spectator,* denounced all visual poetry as "false wit," because he was unable to see that this loss of power and momentum was accompanied by a holistic realism that would make the visual poetry medium suitable for qualities that he did not associate with poetry. Rather the best strategy for the visual poet consists of matching the natural potentials of the medium (or of the intermedium, depending on how one wishes to look at it) with whichever of his or her notions and projections seem most suited for it, and not to try and force it to do something of which it is not capable. The audience, then, sees this process of matching, identifies it, relaxes and enjoys the process. Which is what happy audiences have always done anyway.

*   *   *

Notes

[1] Dick Higgins, *George Herbert's Pattern Poems: In Their Tradition* (West Glover, VT: Unpublished Editions, 1977), pp. 17-19.

[2] Giordano Bruno, *Opera Latine Conscripta.* 3 Vols. in 8 Parts. (1891; Bad Cannstatt b. Stuttgart, Friedrich Frommann Verlag, 1962) v. 1, pt. 3, pp. 87-318, esp. 197-199. In collaboration with Charles Doria I am currently working on the first English translation of this text, for publication in early 1979 by Unpublished Editions.

[3] Isabel Frith, *Life of Giordano Bruno the Nolan,* ed. Prof. Mauriz Carriere (Boston: Ticknor & Company, 1887), p. 16. What Ms. Frith has done is to assemble a montage here of passages from the section referred to in footnote 2.

[4] Higgins, *Op. Cit.,* pp. 10-11.

[5] Christian Wagenknecht, "Proteus and Permutation: Spielarten einer Poetischen Spielart," in *Text und Kritik,* Heft 30 (1970), pp. 1-10.

[6] Etienne Tabourot, *Les Bigarrures du Seigneur des Accords*
1597/1866: Genève: Slatkine Reprints, 1969), p. 113.
[7] Wagenknecht, *Op. Cit.,* p. 6.

Anthologies Referred to in the Text

Jean-François Bory, ed., *Once Again* (New York: New Directions, 1968).

Klaus Peter Dencker, ed., *Text-Bilder: Visuelle Poesie international* (Köln: Dumont Schauberg, 1972).

Mary Ellen Solt, ed., *Concrete Poetry: A World View* (Bloomington: University of Indiana Press, 1970 [1968]).

Emmett Williams, ed., *An Anthology of Concrete Poetry* (New York: Something Else Press, 1967).

PURIFICATION OF LANGUAGE IN MALLARMÉ, DADA AND VISUAL POETRY

Emma Kafalenos

Stéphane Mallarmé's desire to 'purify' language is similar in method to the equally daring literary experiments of Dada and of the contemporary visual poetry movement. The word, for Mallarmé, is a unique and almost living thing which, in its juxtaposition to other unique words, creates the poem. "The pure work," Mallarmé writes, "implies the elocutionary disappearance of the poet, who yields the initiative to the words....they illuminate each other by reciprocal reflections like a virtual train of fire upon jewels" ("Crise de vers," p. 366).[1] This emphasis on the word, and the illumination that results from the juxtaposition of particular words, is what constitutes Mallarmé's method, and that of Dada and visual poetry as well. What we are dealing with above all, as we shall see in each case, is a poetry of the substantive (a noun, or any other part of speech—a gerund for example—that is used as a noun). It is a poetry where the substantive reigns supreme, both in the originality of its selection and in its isolation from its context. In this poetry, substantives that at first seem unrelated to each other are juxtaposed together in such a way that their relationships gradually become apparent in the mind of the reader.

For Mallarmé, particularly in his later poetry, the doctrine of the purification of the word implies a conscious rejection of all the words (and ideas) that are customarily associated with that word—and, as a corollary, it equally implies a search for other words that bear no immediately obvious relationship to the word in question. His later poems thus can be viewed as a series of seemingly unrelated substantives; the semantic relationships between them, which always exist in the case of Mallarmé, can only be determined after careful study. For one of the most extreme examples of this method of composition, let us look at Mallarmé's sonnet written in 1887, "Surgi de la croupe et du bond" (p. 74).

> Surgi de la croupe et du bond
> D'une verrerie éphémère
> Sans fleurir la veillée amère
> Le col ignoré s'interrompt.
>
> Je crois bien que deux bouches n'ont
> Bu, ni son amant ni ma mère,
> Jamais a la même Chimère,
> Moi, sylphe de ce froid plafond!

Le pur vase d'aucun breuvage
Que l'inexhaustible veuvage
Agonise mais ne consent,

Naïf baiser des plus funèbres!
A rien expirer annonçant
Une rose dans les ténèbres.

[Risen from the croup and with a bound
From an ephemeral bit of glass
Without blossoming the bitter evening vigil
The unknown neck stops short.

I do believe that two mouths,
Neither her lover nor my mother,
Have never drunk of the same Chimera,
I, sylph of this cold ceiling!

The pure vase with no potion
Except inexhaustible widowhood
Is dying but consents,

Naive kiss among the most funereal!
To expire nothing announcing
A rose in the shadows.]

Although the central image of the poem is the vase out of which no
rose arises, the nouns of the first line translate from the French as
"croup" (the rump of a horse) and "bound" or "leap"—which in the
context of "croup" must be interpreted (on first reading) as the motion of a horse. Only as we read on, discovering that the image being
evoked is made of glass and does not blossom, do we realize that
"croup" and "bound" refer, respectively, to the shape and to the
élan of the shape of a vertical plane of the vase. Thus the substantives in the first stanza—"croup," "bound," "bit of glass," "blossoming," and "neck" (as unusual as it seems to find them within a single
sentence)—do reflect upon each other, that is, each substantive modifies the meanings of the others, in such a way that the relationships
between and among them can become apparent. The "isolation of
the word," which Mallarmé calls for ("Crise de vers," p. 368) and
which is implied in his rejection of words customarily used together
in one context, is further strengthened by the distortions in his syntax, which critics have often recognized. Even in the first stanza of
this poem, which for Mallarmé is almost straightforward syntactical-
ly, the participial phrase of the first line, which is introduced by "ris-
en," is separated by a full two lines from the noun it modifies, the
"neck" of line four (the translation follows the word order of the

original French almost exactly), thus controlling the slowness of the metamorphosis of the word "croup" from the context of a horse to that of a vase. It should also be noted that there are only four finite verbs in the entire poem—one of which is negated and the others translating as "stops," "is dying," and "expires." The resultant effect is a stasis in which the substantives, silently and without motion, reflect upon each other.

In the poetry of Dada the syntax is generally more straightforward; substantives are usually modified by adjectives and controlled by verbs that agree grammatically, and are often verbs of motion. Dada, unlike Mallarmé's work, is a poetry of motion. But the apparent logic in the syntactical structure of Dada poetry is deceptive. As an example let us look at a poem jointly written by Jean Arp, Walter Serner, and Tristan Tzara, who called themselves the "anonymous society for the exploitation of the dadaist vocabulary." Their poem, "The Hyperbole of the Crocodile's Coiffeur and the Cane," was originally published, in German, in the Dada magazine *Der Zeltweg* in November of 1919:

> das elmsfeuer rast um die bärte der wiedertäufer
> sie holen aus ihren warzen die zechenlampen
> und stecken ihre steisse in die pfützen
> er sang ein nagelknödel auf treibeis
> und pfiff sie so hold um die ecke das lotterliche
> dass ein gussgitter glitschte
> 4 eugens auf tour skandinavien millovitsch blaue kiste
> ist bombenerfolg
> zwischen dem haarrahm des kanalstrotters
> erstiefelte der saumseligste zeisig den breipfahl
> eines buttersackes im zinngefieder
> schreckensfahrt an steiler wand
> der gute vater senket
> ins haupt den tomahwak
> die mutter ruft vollendet
> zum letzten mal ihr quak
> die kinder ziehen reigend
> hinein ins abendrot
> der vater steigt verneigend
> in ein kanonenboot
> auf den marmeladengürtel turnen
> hinein ins abendbrot
> glitzerblöde affenbolde
> wiener hintere zollamtsvokabeln voll grauslichkeit
> der zirkusfeindliche kiel
> hänge das profil

im internationalen
kanäle
abendmahlmarschäl(l)e
quartettmephistophele
skandierskandöle

[the marsh fire rages around the beards of the anabaptists
they are pulling mining lamps from their warts
and sticking their buttocks in puddles
he sang a dumpling stuffed with nails on floating ice
and whistled them so delicately around the corner the slovenly
so that a gutter slides
4 eugens on a tour of scandinavia millovitsch blue box
is a tremendous success
along the line between the forehead and the scalp of the canal trotters
the dilatory siskin stalked along the paddle
of the butter churn in pewter plumage
a journey of horror up a steep wall
the good father sinks
the tomahawk into the head
the mother calls out finished
for the last time her clucking
the children move in a dance
into the evening red
the father climbs bowing
into a gunboat
on the marmalade belt there exercise
into the evening bread
twinklingly stupid ape apers
viennese throaty customsofficevocables full of horror
the circus-hostile keel
should hang the profile
in an international
canals
communion marsha(w)ls
quartet mephistophelian
scanning scandoils]

Dada is above all an experiment in the use of language. In spite of
the relatively traditional syntactical structure, there is experimentation in syntax. Note how many of the lines in this poem (particularly in the last half) can be read in conjunction with either the preceding or the following line, changing the image according to the way
one reads it. Then too, the apparent logic of the syntax in Dada
poetry is deceptive in that the words themselves that form the claus-

es—the subject/predicate units—are not words that are customarily combined in the same clause. The result seems to be that the substantives in this poetry, because of the force of their juxtaposition, reduce the power of the function of the verb, producing a poetry, again, in which the substantive is of foremost importance. Instead of relating the subject of a clause to its complement, and in that way controlling it, the verbs in this poetry seem to function more as modifiers of their subjects, setting them in motion indeed, but in no way controlling their direction.

For clarification, let us look at the beginning of the Arp/Serner/Tzara poem. If the first line were to read "the marsh fire rages above the swamps," the verb "rages," which would convey the power of the fire, would probably be considered at least as important a word as the two substantives. That is, "the marsh fire rages above the swamps" is a much stronger statement than "the marsh fire above the swamps." But let us return to the line as it stands in the poem, juxtaposing the anabaptists' beards and the marsh fire, "the marsh fire rages around the beards of the anabaptists," and then reread the line omitting the verb, "the marsh fire around the beards of the anabaptists." The last version, even with the verb omitted, remains a strong line. Because of the disparity between the images connected by the verbs in this poetry, and the shock of the juxtaposition of the disparate images, the verbs lose their customary relative weight of importance in comparison with the substantives. The verb "rages" in the line we are discussing adds power and motion to the word "fire," but it is only a strengthening of the power and motion already potentially carried by the word "fire." The juxtaposition of "fire" and "beards"—much less anabaptists' beards—is a much stronger element of the line than what is conveyed by the verb "rages."

Thus the effect of this poem, as well as other Dada poetry, is that of a series of substantives, just as it is for Mallarmé. Unlike Mallarmé's substantives, which seem unrelated but whose relationships can be determined with study, the substantives of Dada poetry are often not related in any way that can be perceived. Moreover, unlike the stasis in which Mallarmé's substantives are set—as if they were precious stones—the substantives of Dada are generally in constant and rapid motion. What we do find in Dada that is similar to Mallarmé is a series of customarily unrelated substantives juxtaposed together, and carrying the excitement of the poem in the very shock of their juxtaposition. Even in their stated purposes Mallarmé and Dada show similarities. The Dada attempt to "shock the bourgeoisie" and, more importantly, to find a new language for poetry that has not become trite through centuries of use, nor distorted through the political slogans of World War I, is not very different from Mallarmé's despair that poetry alone of all the arts is without its arcana—that it is "without mystery against hypocritical curiosity, without terror against the impious, or under the smile and grimace of the ignorant and the enemy" ("L'Art pour tous," p. 257).

In the visual poetry movement, which claims Mallarmé as an influence (particularly for the typographical experiments of *Un coup de dés*), syntax often disappears entirely, being replaced by spatial relationships which provide the structure traditionally created by syntax. The Dadaist Kurt Schwitters, who is better known (perhaps wrongly) for his visual collages than for his poetry and his theoretical writings, recognized the similarity in structure that already existed between Dada poetry and Dada collages. Writing in 1924, Schwitters considered traditional poetry organized according to the "association of ideas." Discussing what he terms "abstract poetry" (which probably refers both to the Dada poems composed of words with semantic meanings with which we are concerned here, and to Dada sound poems that are devoid of semantic meaning), he continues:

> Abstract poetry released the word from its associations—this is a great service—and evaluated word against word and in particular, concept against concept. . .The end pursued by abstract poetry is pursued, logically, by Dadaist painters, who, in their pictures, evaluate object against object by sticking or nailing them down side by side.[2]

The juxtaposition of word against unassociated word, then, or concept against unassociated concept in the Dada poem—within the framework of traditional syntax—was already at the time seen as similar to the juxtaposition of object against unassociated object in the Dada collage—where spatial relationships took the place of syntax.

The large majority of visual poems are composed of one or more substantives. The spatial arrangement of the word or words on a page suggests potential meanings embedded in a single word, and also the sometimes unexpected relationships that can be found between words that are juxtaposed within a poem. John Sharkey's "Schoenberg" was composed of a single word, the name of the composer Schoenberg.[3]

The spacing of the letters on the page and the size of the letters (particularly the two adjacent large b's in the seventh and eighth lines, which introduce the "berg") remind us of the meanings of the two syllables as separate words; in German "schoen" and "berg" translate as "beautiful mountain." The variation in the size of the letters in the poem can be interpreted as a notation of volume in a polyphonic score. Thus the very tiniest letters, apparently mere dots, are probably rests indicating silence—suggesting the pointillistic technique that characterizes the later compositions of Schoenberg and those of his immediate followers.

A poem composed of several substantives, and depending on their juxtaposition for its meaning, is Paul de Vree's "The Clock of Modernity."[4]

O

TI   VI

RAGE

CI   MI

GA

Written in French, the poem is shaped like a clock—and also a wheel
with spokes, or an unusually complex intersection. At the center is
the French "rage," which translates as "rage" or "madness." Surrounding it are six prefixes each of which, when followed by "rage,"
forms a substantive. In English, clockwise from the top, the words
are: storm, a turning (of a car), mirage, garage (or parking), waxing,
and (the sixth) both hauling (as in a truck) or a drawing (in a lottery).
Each of these words contributes to our understanding of their
shared element "rage"—the madness of modern life. Visual poetry,
like Dada poetry, conforms to Mallarmé's definition of the "pure
work"; words "illuminate each other by reciprocal reflections." In
each case words, usually substantives, acquire new aspects of meaning
as a result of their placement together in a poem.

It is this juxtaposition of substantives, as well as the response of the reader to such juxtapositions, that constitute the similarity between the works of Mallarmé, Dada, and visual poetry. It is the image, composed of the substantive, which functions with the support of traditional syntax, as the conveyor of the idea. For Mallarmé, "to choose an object and disengage from it a state of the soul" is to create the symbol ("Enquête de Jules Huret," p. 869). It is the open-ended nature of the symbol, as Mallarmé uses it, that is indicative of the way we must read all these poets. Unlike the metaphor which rests on two fixed meanings, the symbol, for Mallarmé, rests upon the assigned meaning of the image; its other meanings are not absolute. As John Unterecker puts it, the "symbol stands on one leg only; the other kicks at the stars."[5] The result is that the Mallarmé poem is re-created in the mind of the reader—and is a somewhat different poem in the minds of different (and equally competent) readers, because the unassigned interpretations of the images, and the relationships between the images always vary to some degree from reader to reader. Whether we speak of the symbol in Mallarmé, or simply the image in Dada, or reduce our terminology even farther to refer to the substantive in visual poetry, we find in all these works the substantive (of which the image is composed) or the image (of which the symbol is composed) given without an absolute interpretation within the poem. The reader in every case, under the shock of the juxtaposition of these substantives or images, must interpret the poem by contemplating the images, in order to perceive the relationships between them— the unwritten relationships which the reader re-establishes for himself and which for him become his experience of the poem.

[1] *Oeuvres complètes,* ed. Henri Mondor and G. Jean-Aubry (Paris: Gallimard, Bibliothèque de la Pléiade, 1945). Subsequent quotations from Mallarmé's writings are identified, within parentheses in the text, by the title of the article and the page number in this edition. All translations are mine.

[2] "Logically Consistent Poetry," quoted in English by Hans Richter, *Dada: Art and Anti-Art* (New York: McGraw-Hill, 1965), pp. 148-149.

[3] *Once Again,* ed. Jean-François Bory (New York: New Directions, 1968), p. 16.

[4] Paul de Vree, *Zimprovisaties* (Antwerp: De Tafelronde, 1968), p. 42.

[5] *A Reader's Guide to William Butler Yeats* (New York: Noonday, 1959), p. 34.

VISUAL POETRY REFLECTED

POETRY IS THE COFFIN OF LANGUAGE

INSIDE THE COFFIN IS A MIRROR

THE EYE AND THE WORD (IN ADDITION
TO EVERYTHING ELSE) ARE JOINED IN
THE INSTANT, OR DEATH, OF CREATION

VISUAL POETRY (IS NOT MOST POETRY
IN SOME MEASURE A VISUAL RECORD
AND EXPERIENCE?)
IS IN THE EYE SMEARS ON THE MIRROR
OF DEATH

JOHN M. BENNETT   1978

VISUAL WRITING FORMS IN ANTIQUITY:
THE *VERSUS INTEXTI*

Charles Doria

The letter "A" is usually taken as a visual abstraction of the four or five ways of saying or hearing the first vowel. That is, "A" is a symbol, the perceptible portion of a partially unknown, possibly unknowable concept or relationship. As such, it almost denotes, if it does not define, the modern notion of reading: from sensory stimulation (eye/ear) to brain and then back out again. But letter "A" has lost its graphic character, and I think the gradual streamlining and simplifying over centuries of the design of the alphabet's letters reflect the movement of attention away from the letter as glyph or quick ("sign") picture and, because letters are combined into words, into the sensory and cognitive areas of the brain.

But the source of the letter "A" is a picture—of a bull with horns: Aleph the Bull.[1] In astrology the sign is still used, known there as Taurus. In Galenic Signs (another adaptation of our source script, Phoenician Letters, still used by chemists and druggists, definitively collected and defined, according to tradition, by Galen the Physician in the 2nd century C.E.), aleph reappears, with the female cross appended, as the sign for Mercury.[2] In fact, Galenic Signs can be arranged to tell a little story, as Rudolf Koch did in *Book of Signs*.[3] This narration with signs allows us to reexperience our lettering, in a slightly altered way, in something more like their original earlier character—as pictograms. But as it happened, Phoenician Letters progressed from being pictograms to syllable and phoneme markers, until sometime among the Greeks they became denoters of individual marks—"letters" in our sense of the word.

This closeness between the word as composition and representation, between what it does and what it wears (its shape or visual uniqueness), was something felt throughout Antiquity. In the first century B.C.E. Varro, perhaps the first person ever to write a book on language, in a passage that deserves to be better known, decribes and explains the condition as follows:

> For a person can *facere* (make) something and not *agere* (do) it, as a poet *facit* 'makes' a play and does not act it, and on the other hand the actor *agit* 'acts' it and does not make it, and so a play *fit* 'is made' by the poet, not acted, and *agitur* 'is acted' by the actor, not made. . . .
> In its literal sense *facere* 'to make' is from *facies* 'external appearance' on the thing which he *facit* 'makes.' As the *fictor* 'image-maker,' when he [the Formator—the poet?] says *"Formo* 'I form,' " puts a *forma* 'form [also: beauty—cf. the Greek *tō kalon* 'the beautiful is the structured']' on it, so when he says *"Facio* 'I make,' " he puts a *facies* 'ex-

ternal appearance' on it. . . .for he who *dicit* 'says' something, we say
facere 'makes' words, and he who *agit* 'acts' something, we say is not *in-
ficiens* 'failing to do' something.

(*On the Latin Language,* vi. 77-78, R.G. Kent, trans.)

Varro suggests a union of both nature and semantics between the
doing (*facere*) and the thing done (*facies*). But *facies* also conveys
"form, appearance, face," so a development to shaped poetry represents both a literal unfolding and an explanation of the process of
poetry—from creation to the creation.

One kind of visual poem is called *versus intexti,* 'woven verses,'
grids or word-squares with texts running horizontally ('the woof')
and vertically ('the warp'), usually metered.[6] The contemporary
scholars Caruso and Polara in their *Iuvenilia Loeti* (Rome, 1969) attempt a more precise definition:

> The technique of the *versus intexti* [consisted of the following] : not only
> was the number of the letters in each line of verse fixed and immutable, but
> some letters were obligatory. Composition proceeded like this: the page was
> usually divided into 1225 small squares (35x35); a figure was traced by means
> of words whose large patterned letters fill up their squares. Around and
> through these lines the verses were written in smaller letters, beginning in this
> way to fill up the entire page, and at this point one passes finally to the com-
> position of the actual, real lines of verse, filling the remaining empty holes
> with letters that form words that give meaning to the whole text.

Most *versus intexti* follow the same theme, which is also that of
their inception. The poet asks the mercy, or the favor, of a lord:
either the Christian god or his visible agent in temporal affairs, the
Christian emperor. For this is the situation that the reputed inventor
of *versus intexti,* Publilius Optatianus Porfyrius (usually known now-
adays as Optatian and not to be confused with Porphyrius, the Neo-
platonist also in the third century, or Porphyrion, a commentator on
Horace) wove around his invention. To secure his return from banishment, he sent a small collection of *versus intexti* as a gift to Constantine, the first of the Christian emperors, after he had ascended to the
imperiate following his victory over (and death of) his rival Maxentius
in 312 at the Milvian Bridge just outside of Rome.

According to then-current accounts, Constantine and his troops
were inspired before this battle by a vision of the cross as a chrismon[4]
emblazoned with:

> *in hoc signo vince*
> ("in this sign conquer")

As a result, Constantine's army all wore one or the other popular
monogram for Christ on their uniforms. Constantine himself used the
sign, called the 'chrismon'

which is a Greek *X* ("chi") superimposed on a *P* ("rho"), the first two
letters of *Chr*ist, on the *labarum,* his official war banner, and later, on
official documents and inscriptions, attributing to it his victory and
subsequent reign. And, of course, the chrismon figures prominently
in Optatian's *versus contexti* to the emperor. The practice of using
monograms[5] (from the Greek *monogramma,* meaning "single letter,"
which may for our purposes be defined as combining the letter
strokes and shapes of a word, name, or phrase to form a single shape
or sign) was followed by later Holy Roman Emperors, ninth- and
tenth-century Teutonic-Papal imitations of the successors of Augus-
tus, like Charlemagne and Otto the Great. Other monograms, involving Christ and Gospel terms, were current at this time. I see in their
invention a parallel with the Galenic Signs discussed earlier, and it is
tempting to consider this intense interest in signs from the third to the
sixth centuries C.E. as popular, communal anticipation of the coming
cultural and lingual fragmentation that followed the final collapse of
the Roman Empire in the West in the sixth century.

From that time dates the ascendancy of sign and image as "talking
picture" (as in stained glass or mural sequences) or as part of the language (the letters themselves perhaps) of the medieval *librum naturae*
(book of nature, here conceived as a set of divine, verifiable metaphors for Christian typology and theology—St. Patrick's reading of the
shamrock as the trinity would be one such instance). This period of
sign and signification, I believe, is an outgrowth of the need that was
felt then to hide, store, concentrate, epitomize complex concepts and
thoughts, as well as other important items of cultural in-formation,
against a time of confusion and disruption, as the Early Middle Ages
(600 - 1000) undoubtedly were. Sign and signification also reflect
the need for a new kind of literacy to replace declining Latin and
Greek.

In light of all this, it is no wonder Constantine welcomed Optatian's poetic advent and his *versus intexti.* They were to be taken as
a literary enshrining of the important symbol and power sign of C's
imperium, the chrismon. By the very process of shaping verse into
an overarching, informing sign, monogram, or form, often Christian
in inspiration, one could glimpse a visionary showing-forth of God's
hand, intervening and operating through the emperor, his earthly representative, who, through the etiquette and adulation of the imperial court, could also be seen as God's avatar, mirroring Him in the As-
sembly of the Saints receiving obeisance.

By weaving C's chrismon into *versus intexti,* Optatian manipulated another powerful Roman symbol: the imperium as *lex* (law—literally "a reading" as when one reads the decrees of the Senate or the emperor in order to render authoritative judgment, deciding issues as if the Senate or the emperor were there in person on the spot, executing decision and sentence; for by the principle of *lex* one thought and acted in their names and used their words, their language, as interpreted, almost as an omen, from the appropriate statute or regulation).

The process that Optatian discovered, of ordering shape by rigidly controlling letter and image, corresponds as well to the Roman desire to see event—history—as pattern subject to divine intervention, foreordained for the ultimate good of the State (Vergil's understanding of Fate in the *Aeneid*): intervention, in other words, issuing from the emperor and his court, thought of as those potent but conserving signs, that can be discerned everywhere in time's welter, in the woof of reality. This image approaches, if it does not exactly replicate, the three spinning Fates of Greek religion, Clotho, Lachesis and Atropos, who respectively weave, twist into shape, and finally sever the threads of every individual existence. Further, in Optatian's use of the chrismon, he identifies the crucifix (or Christ) as the sign that won the emperor his throne. No more potent magic could be asked. Note that in Latin the word for poem, *carmen,* also means magic charm or incantation; and by etymology, *carmen* still does.

Constantine's response to *versus intexti* was intense. He even took the unusual step, for a Roman emperor, of writing (or having a scribe write for him to sign) the poet a Commendatory Letter, which fortunately survives. Among other things, the emperor tells the poet:

It has been my pleasure [to note] that ability in your studies attains this degree of excellence: that it creates new forms for composing [arranging?] verse while it observes the ancient practices [i.e., the poems, following models already 300 or more years old, were metered in dactylic hexameter, the epic line of Vergil, Statius, Lucan, to name some poets of the imperial court, and respected classical canons regarding language and diction, so that they exhibited stylistic and thematic continuity with the Caesarian past of patronage of and glorification through literature, especially poetry and history.—C.D.]
Most writers fail to reach a level of competency whereby they are able to compose a poem without technical faults, all defects eliminated, since they are bound, so to speak, by the nodes [i.e., the thorny mechanical and metrical problems] of their art.
To you—despite the difficulty which arises from the letter count [total number of characters in each line], from the lines traced by the verses as they crisscross the center of the poesis [here the Roman emperor used a Greek word *poiesis,* which in that language literally means, according to Liddell and Scott's dictionary: "a making, fabrication, a creating" as in the 'poiesis of ships' (Thucydides), the 'poiesis of images' (Sophocles), while in Latin it means all this, as well as the craft, or study, of poetry and the result of the poetic process—a finished poem.], which you intended to make [*facere*] in such a way that the figures in different colors [Op-

tatian used different colored inks for thread] would please the eye, it also
fell to your happy lot to succeed in this purpose: that your revealing to
sight of modes, or patterns [the chrismon and the other inwoven, intervening signs—C's word here is *norma,* "a rule, pattern, precept," which originally denoted the carpenter's T square] , did not prove a hindrance to the
poiesis. For this reason I thank you for your gift. It [the poetry] demonstrates the training and discipline of your mind and your natural gift [for
poetry—word-making—in this double sense] .

Constantine's genuine belief that something in *versus intexti* intrigued him—that they hypostasized attitudes and events that marked
and assisted him in his rise to power, where as emperor he could both
initiate and control pattern through *lex* (his laws and decrees) and
hex (sign in letter shape as personal and divine manifestation) in his
name and God's—comes through very well here. Especially significant is the wording "for this reason" at the beginning of the second
to last sentence. Constantine is officially affirming in a state docu-
ment that the reason why he wishes to thank the poet, among other
things, but perhaps most of all, is that the figures stitched in the verse
lines do not interfere with the normal flow of the words—surely a
conscious image or description of what impact the emperor hoped
his rule, here considered the warp or the sign (the chrismon), would
have on the empire, here the woof, the lines of verse which read
from left to right with their traditionally hallowed invocations and
suppliant prayers. For the verses represent, almost in a physical
sense, the cultural continuum of the Mediterranean that every poem
in some sense intersects simply by being born and thus in-forms.
In fact, the very triteness of Optatian's hexameter lines in the *versus intexti,* their obvious unoriginality of word and sentiment, both
witnesses and executes his intention not to impede the movement of
the older poetic form, but to abide by its customs and conventions, re-
specting it in an impersonal and formulaic manner strangely reminis-
cent of Homeric fidelity to communally constructed, time- and oral-
proven methods of verse crafting, even while Optatian honors the ancient, 'pagan' notions of taste and stylistic excellence in poetry.
Imaginative focus now shifts, in the *versus intexti,* from making poems
(*facere verba* or *versus*) to *facies* (the made shape or appearance, as
Varro puts it—the face—the home-grown Latin equivalent of Greek
poiesis discussed earlier). Putting it another way, Optatian, by wedding
the new and untried to the old in such a way that new signs and forms
take root, in-forming the old verse forms and meters, without doing
violence to traditional ways, to traditional language and art (i.e., culture), both reveals and reflects the exact nature of Constantine's imperium, which attempted to bridge and unify both classical past and
oncoming Judeochristian universalism with its attendant, imperial-
theological rhetoric. Consider once again, but in this context, Constantine's remark that he finds pleasure in the poet's poems be-

cause they are "new forms for composing [arranging?] verse" while
they observe "the ancient practices": just as Constantine, in his Edict
of Milan in 328, began the establishment of Christianity as the state religion while proclaiming official tolerance for all older cults and faiths,
including the Olympian religion. What has in fact happened is that
Optatian's poiesis and Constantine's imperium have become nearly
identical mirrors of each other, in that realm where ideas, realities,
and volition are given a figured representation, under the aegis of artistic imagination and underlying cultural fact.

Constantine and his successors were quick to see all this in *versus
intexti* and to honor it significantly: hence the emperor's Commendatory Letter to the poet, and the many later instances of royal patronage of Optatian's epigones. For the emperor—whether Roman or
Holy Roman—understood that his historical uniqueness and significance had been literally captured in Optatian's new art form, express-
ly invented to impress Constantine, and which, not surprisingly, failed
to survive the decline of the Holy Roman Empire.

In the *versus intexti* of Optatian and those who came after him,
like Josephus Scotus of Charlemagne's court, visual and oral stresses
were either identical or disregarded as if incidental, hence subordinate,
to the main purpose and signification of the poem.[6] But towards the
end of the imperial period, in the ninth and tenth centuries, the poets
began distorting,[7] and later even suppressing, the verse woof, while
preserving the regularity and orderliness of the figured warp. This development, I think, reflects real difficulties the imperial idea was en-
countering and the emperor's failing ability to intervene in the pattern, to control event by lex and hex; it also reflects the breakdown
of the imperial model itself. No longer was it possible to view the emperor as a sacred king, granting the ancient culture sanctuary in the
straightness and deliberately unoriginal tolerance of his rule while he
promotes God's intervention on earth, instructing his imperium by
sign and demeanor into a truer knowledge and understanding of the
divine topology.

For example, Bernowin the Bishop,[8] somewhere called the Homer
of the ninth-century Carolingian court, creates an awry, moiré fabric
in one of his *versus intexti* by breaking and stretching the verse lines
through and against the superimposed vertical text (which consists of
DEUS MISERERE, "God, have mercy," repeated five times—a sacred
reworking of Optatian's pleas to Constantine for revocation of banishment and recall to the imperial court, except that Bernowin wishes to
be redeemed from sin (banishment from Eden) and summoned to the
Heavenly Court). His text here, however, is more hectic, 'inspired,'
than any of the self-consciously trite Optatian:

> May Christ the Lord, of Jesse's seed, give, yes give,
> eternal life to little me since He is Himself eternal

and vital life, Jesus, both Victor and Victory, You
are forever, sempiternal and immediate [*simul*], You alone
are life-bestowing, are kind, have mercy on me and mercy
on my sins, You are the just Judge, just are Your judgments
of me Your servant, You alone are salvation, hope, You alone
are faith enduring forever, You are right and fitting,
raised on high, You seek the lofty/the excellent, Retributor,
repair the matter (of my salvation), pius King, Redeemer,
good Founder of the Church of churches, You are Yourself
the Purchaser of sin, King of kings, the Ruler, Guider
and Lover of kingdoms: rescue your little one, save your
(Bernowin) poor and needy everywhere.

The graph below illustrates further the distentions and cross-stresses
of this last poem. *Visual and oral stresses in Bernowin XI*

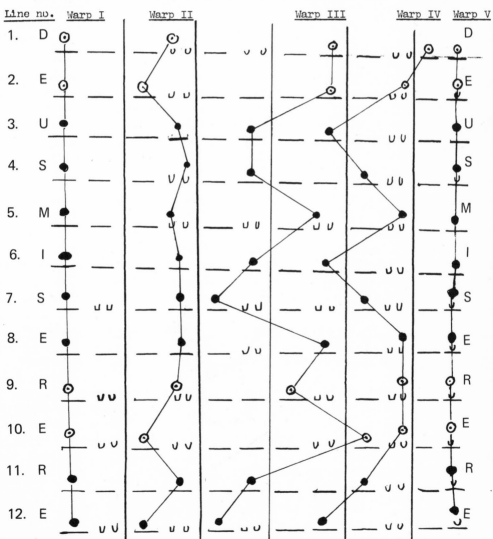

Meter: dactylic hexameter with spondaic substitution. Elisions not shown.

Key

— = long syllable with a time value of 2

U = short syllable with a time value of 1

⏑ = long-short syllable, conventionally treated
      as having a time value of 2

● = unstressed syllable of the vertical text

☉ = stressed syllable of the vertical text

   This shows what I earlier referred to as its moiré effect: as if spun in silk, the glabrous threads of the poem fail to make orderly contact with each other, and the vertical, 'imperial' text molds into procrustean equality the anguished cry of the horizontal, 'audible,' text.

   Later *versus intexti* dispense with verse-woof entirely:[9] the empire is slowly coming unglued from its embedding matrix in historical time, losing its ability to in-form. But the verbal form shines through the whiteness of the page all the more clearly, like an idea in the void, not allowed to take shape, or intervene in written form, in the otherwise seamless rush of events. And so ends this brief history of a fairly unknown writing form—many would hesitate to call it part of Literature—that abandoned the traditional resources of poetry in service and search of signs, thus returning written language, for a while, to its point of origin—pictogram and hieroglyph.

NOTES & ILLUSTRATIONS

1a

A, alpha, aleph the bull: Taurus: April

Ib   Common Galenic Signs

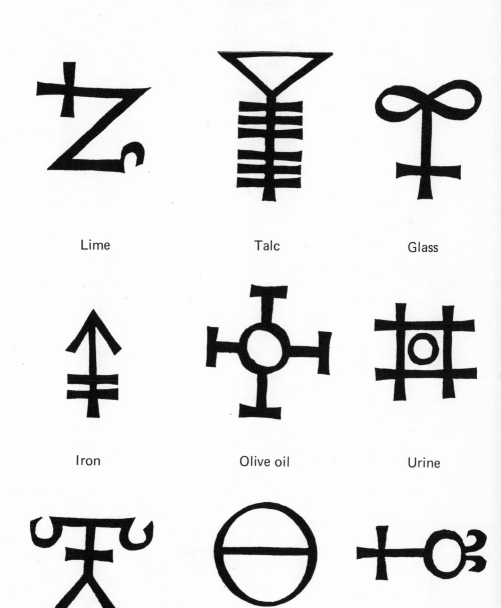

Lime   Talc   Glass

Iron   Olive oil   Urine

Lead   Salt   Alcohol or wine

2

Alpha Beth: Bull Woman:
Mercury, planet and metal:
ManWoman, the Hermaphrodite

3

man   woman

fuck

preggers   one child born

family, man woman (2) kids

men fight

man dies

men friends

woman with two kids

one child dies

one child left

woman dies

child with centering seed

—adapted from R. Koch, *The Book of Signs*

4   Chrismons or monograms on the name "Jesus Christ"

a. The Gnostic Sun Wheel, adapted as an early chrismon

b

A pagan Sun Wheel, containing a Greek *X* (chi) and *I* (iota), Christ's initials.

c

A proposed visual 'etymology' for the chrismon: a Sun Wheel mounting above a crucifix, signifying Christ's death and eventual resurrection. If the wheel and cross were joined, the Galenic Sign for woman would be formed:

In astrology, this sign denotes Venus; in chemistry, copper. Was the
relationship between the womb and copper known to ancient medi-
cine? Note as well its surely not unintentional resemblance to the
aleph/Mercury/hermaphrodite sign shown earlier.

d. A monogram of Jesus, containing, the first three letters of his name
in Greek: *I* (iota), *H* (eta = long 'e'), *S* (sigma). The Romans interpreted this monogram, or read it, as Latin initial slang for *In hoc signo
(vince)*, the same phrase that occurred in the vision of the chrismon
Constantine and his troops witnessed. It was also read as:

*I*esus	Jesus
*H*ominum	Humanity's
*S*alvator	Savior

In grade school, I learned it as "*I have suffered*," Christ's last words
on the cross.

Variations of the chrismon

e

The chrismon as Constantine knew it: a Greek *X* (chi) super-imposed on an *P* (rho): the first two letters of *Chr*ist in Greek.

Here the *X* has changed to a *T* (tau), a crucifix.

In this one, the *X* has changed to a shepherd's crook—or bish-op's mitre: either a reference to Christ as the Good Shepherd or to his church's episcopacy— or a possible allusion to the crux ansata

The chrismon as an inverted crux ansata, the sign of Isis, or of the ever-fecund cunt of the Nile (cf. the biblical expression "land of Cush [or cunt]" for Egypt.)

A chrismon as eight Greek *X*'s —an instance of a concealed chrismon.

Two chrismons based on an alpha (left) and an omega (right), a visual translation of Christ's statement that he is 'alpha and omega, beginning and end.'

A chrismon inside a crux ansata: in astrology the sign for the Earth

A triple chrismon, with three *P*'s of varying heights superimposed
on each other. Note the three alphas and three omegas on the right
and left. Trinitarian symbolism (3x3x3)—but the repetition of elements, as often happens in Antiquity, is also there for emphasis.
Found in a Roman catacomb.

Some names in monogram from late Antiquity 5a

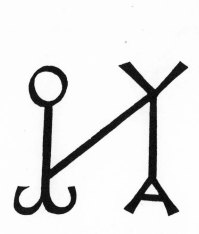

Ioannes (John)   Nikolaus

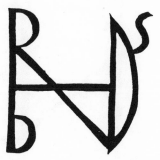

Areobindus

Arkadius   Paulos

Two christian expressions in monogram form   5b

Vivas in deo — "May you live in God."

Bene valete — "Fare well" or "Stay strong [in the Lord]."

5c   Various imperial monograms

Justinian   Palaeologus
the Lawgiver

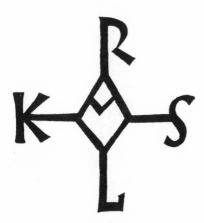

Pipin the Short

"Karolus"
(Charlemagne)

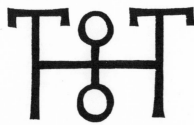

Otho the Great

Five examples of Optatianus' word squares 35x35 letters; the
second two contain as part of the ground the giant capitals 'chi-rho',
the first two letters of Christ in Greek: the chrismon.

6a

```
      5        10        15        20        25        30        35
   M A R T I A·GE S T A·M O D I S·A V D A X·I M I T A T A·SO N O R I S
   M V S A·P E·RE F F I G I E M·T V R M A R V M·C A R M I NA T E X I T
   E·T·N V N C·AG M E N·A G I T·Q V I N O·S V B·L I M I T E·R E C T V M
   M V S I G E·NO·S P A T I V M·S E P T E N O·M I L I T E·DI S T A N S
   N V N·C·E A·DE M·V E R S O·R E L E G E N S·V T C V M Q·VE·M E A T V
   M I T T I T·IN·A M F R A C T V S·N O N·V N A·L E G E·CA T E R V A S
   DISSONA·C O M P O N I·D I V E R S O·C A R M I N E·GAVDENS
   GR A T A N I·MI S·F L E X V·D O C I L I·D E·P E R P E·T E·M E T RO
   O·RS A·I T E R·VM·F I N I·S O C I A N S·C O N F I NI A·C O N T RA
10 P R·AE P O N E N·SO R S·I S·N V L L O·D I S C R I M I N E·M E T R I
   Q V I·NE T I A M·PA R T E S·M E D I A E·S V A·MV N I A·D O CT A E
   E X P E·DI V N T·V E·RS I S·V I C I B V S·N·AM F I N E·S E·D V N O
   Q V A M V·I S·A M B I G·VO S·C V R S V S·E·T·D E V I A·CLA V D I T
   O S T E N T·AN S·A R T E M·VINCIRES·C R V P E A·PR A E B E T
15 S A R M A T I·CA S·S V M·ME S·T R A G E·SE T·T O T A·P E R A C T A
   V O T A·P R E C·OR F A·VE A S·S V B·C E R T O·C O·ND I T A·V I S V
   F A C T O R V M·G·NA R V M·T A M·G R A N D I A·DI C E R E·V A T E M
   I A M·T O T I E N S·AV G V S T E·L I C E T·C A·MP O N A·C R V O R E
   H O S T I L I·P O·ST B E L L A·M A D E N S·ART I S S I M A·T O T O
20 C O R P O R A·FV S A·SO L O S·V B M E R S·AS·A M·NE R E P L E T O
   V I C T R I X·MI R E T V·RT V R B A S·A·CI E M Q V E·FE R O C E M
   P L V R I M A·C O N A R E·RPHOEBEO·C A R M I N E·GA V D E N S
   M A R G E N S·I S·M E M·OR A R E·B O N I·C·AE L E S T I A·FA C T A
   I N T R·OI T V S·E T·BE L L A·L O Q V I·P E·RC V L S A·R·VI N I S
25 Q V I S·DE V I C T·A·I A C E T·G E N S·D V R O·MA R T E·C·AD V C A
   T E·ST I S·M A G·NO R V M·V I C I N A·B O N O N I·A·PR A E S·EN S
   S·I T·V O T I·C·OM P O S·E X C I S·A Q V E·A G M I·NA C E R N E·NS
   DE T·I V G A·CA P T I V I S·E T·D V C A T·C E T E R A·PR A E D A·S
   GRANDIA·V I C T O R I·M O L I M V R·P R O E L I A·PLECTRO
30 D I C E R E·NE C·S A T I S·E S T·V O T V M·S I·C O M P·LE A·T O R E
   M V S A·S V·OQ V A E C V M Q V E·P A R A T·S V B·L E G E·SO N A R E
   S C R V P O·SI S·I N N E X A·M O D I S·P E R F E C T A·CA M E N I S
   V V L T·R E·SO N A R E M E I S·E T·T E S T I S·N O T A·TR O P A E A
   D E P I C T·IS·S I G N A R E·M E T R I S·C V M·M V N E·RE S·A C R O
35 M E N T I S·DE V O T A E·P L A C A R I N T·F A T A·PR O C E L L A S
```

6b

```
                5        10        15        20        25        30        35
    S A N C T E·D E C V S·M V N D I·A C R E R V M·S V M M A·S A L V T I S
    L·V X·P I A·T E R R A R V M·T E S O L O·P R I N C I P E S·A E C L I S
    I N M E N S V M·G A V D E R E·B O N I S·D A T V R·A V R E A·V E N I T
    S V M M O·M I S S A·D E O·F V S I S·P A T E R·A L M E·T Y R A N N I S
 5  V S T I T I A·I N·T E R R A S·E T·G L O R I A·C A N D I D A·V E R I
    T E Q V E·D V C E·M A G E·G R A T A·F I D E S·E T·I V R A·H E N A T A
    T O T A Q V E·P E R C V L S I S·I N G E N T I·M O L E·T Y R A N N I S
    A S P E R A V I S·P O S I T A E S T·B E L L I·R E S·I T A L A·I V R E
    S C E P T R A·D A B I T·P O P V L I S·V O T O·P I V S·O R B I S·E O I
10  A V G V S T E·I N·V I C T A S·M V N D I·T R A N S I B I S·I N·O R A S
    T E Q V E S·V P L E X·T O T I S·D V C I B V S·S T I P A T A S·Y E N E
    O R A T·I V R A·C V P I T·L V C I S·S I B I·G A V D I A·N O S T R A E
    O P T A T A·M A T·F A L L A X·E N·P E R F I D A·T E L A·F V G A R V M
    P A R T H V S·D E P O S V I T·R V I T O R I S·V N D I Q V E·R V B R I
15  L I T O R I S·A E T H E R I O E N·V T V·C E R T A M I N E·A M O R I S
    M E D V S·A R A B S·M O X·O M N I S·O V A T·L A V D A R E·S E R E N I
    O R I S·L V S T R A T V·I D A T·V E R I S·S A N C T E·T R O P A E I S
    H A E C·M A G E·F E L I C E S·T I T V L O S·V T·V I N C A S·A M O R E
    A V R E A·P E R P E T V O R E S·T A V R A N S·S A E C V L A·M V N D O
20  I N D V S·E T·A V R O R A E M·I L E S·Q V O S·F L V M I N E·N I L V S
    T A N G I T·F E C V N D I S·V E N T V R V S·F R V G I F E R·V N D I S
    O R A N T E S·P I A·I V R A·P E T E N T·G E N S·N O B I L I S·O R T V
    A E T H I O P E S·C V N C T I·P A R E N T·O P T A T A Q V E·M V N D I
    T E M P O R A·L A E T A·D E D I T·N O B I S·F E L I C I T A S·A E V I
25  E N S V P L I C E S·P E R S A E·I V R A·S I B I·R E G I A·N O L V N T
    T E·D O M I N V M·M A L V N T·F V S I·T V A S·E M P E R·A D O R A N T
    O R A S·V I S C V P I V N T·T O T I S·T I B I·C E D E R E·R E G N I S
    T V·P I V S·E T·I V S T I·V E R E·M E M O R·I N C L Y T E·L A E T I S
    D A R E S P O N S A·B O N O S·E M P E R·M I T I S S I M V S·O R B I S
30  I M P E R·T I R E T·V V M·C L E M E N T E R·E T·A D D I T O N·V M E N
    S I N T·M A G E·F E L I C E S·P A R I T E R·Q V O S·A L M E·T V E R E
    E T·R E P A R A T A·I V G A N S·M A E S T I·D I V O R T I A·M V N D I
    O R B E S·I V N G E·P A R E S·D E T·L E G E S·R O M A·V O L E N T I S
    P R I N C I P E T E·I N·P O P V L O S·M I T T I·F E L I C I V S·A E V O
35  O M N I A·L A E T E N T V R·F L O R E N T I B V S·A V R E A·R E B V S
```

Optatian's *versus intexti* for the emperor Constantine with the chrismon inwoven.

```
        5      10        15        20        25        30        35
   OQVI·TARTAREA·SPEDE·FAVCES·PROTERIS·ALMO
   O·MISERATE·TVOSQVIS·IGNEA·TEMPLA·SVPREMI
   ANNVISSE·POLI·PIA·LVCIS·REGNA·PATERNAE
   TV·VIRTVS·AETERNA·DEI·TECVM·OMNIA·CHRISTE
 5 TVNC·PATER·EXORSVS·CVM·MOLE·OBSITA·PIGRO
   SQVALORE·EMERSIT·POSITO·QADRISIT·OPERTO
   ANTEOR·TVS·HOMINVM·SANCTO·TVDIVE·TONANTI
   SECRETA·EVIRES·QVEM·TVTVM·MENS·GENITORIS
   SOLA·TENENS·PRVDENS·QDEI·DEVS·INTERIORIS
10 PRINCIPII·SOBOLEM·NVLLIVS·VASTA·CRVENTO
   QVODMORS·REGNABAT·LETORATA·GAVDIA·FVDIT
   ORE·MEDELLIFERO·NEC·POENA·PERPETE·FRANGI
   DEPVLSOS·HOMINES·PLACVIT·NATALIB:ASTRIS
   TVM·TV·PROSTRATIS·VITAE·VIA·SED·TAMEN·OLIM
15 PRAESAGO·ADMONITV·TE·VATVM·FATA·CANEBANT
   TEQVIA·FECVNDVS·PORRO·ORTVS·ERRORA·GEBAT
   CONSILII·VT·SVMMAM·RERVM·SATORE·DIDITORE
   O·VERE·PATRIS·SAPIENTIA·CHRISTE·OPVLENTO
   EXERTVS·VERBO·DE·TRVSVM·IN·VINCVLA·MORTIS
20 MOX·HOMINEM·SVMIS·QVAEQ:EST·VISVNA·SALVTI
   INFIMA·DIGNARE·QVOD·NATVRAE·ORDINE·RECTO
   VT·PERCVLSA·LEVES·INCLINEREIPSE·IACENTI
   NON·E·TERRENO·CORPVS·TIBI·PONDERE·TRACTVM
   PRAECELSO·SED·VIRGO·VTERVM·DE·SEMINE·FETA
25 NEC·SEGNI·COITV·NATVS·SED·CON·IVGE·CAELOES
   CORPOREVS·VVLTV·DEV·SACTV·CASVS·VTRVMQVE
   INVITANS·IVSSA·EXEM·PLIS·HOMINIQ:DICATVS
   AEQVALIS·DOMINVS·QV·IALIS·ONEROSA·CADVCO
   DICTAS·ITHVMANOS·PEREM·VT·DIVINA·IMITATV
30 I·PSE·HOMINIS·TITVLO·INCEDISTEQ:PROFANIS
   MAXIME·IVDAEIS·PLECTENDVM·POST·PIA·MILLE
   MVNIA·PERMITTIS·LET·VMQVES·ALVBRELVISTI
   MONXNECA·THVMANAS·INSECARO·PENDVLANO·XAS
   ATEPATER·INSEDESNAT·VMRECIPITQVEVEHITQ
35 AETERNVM·SALVISSIGN·VM·DAT·MACHINA·SACRA
```

Another of Optatian's *versus intexti* for Constantine, with an inwoven chrismon, as in the preceding example. Note that this one uses a mirror or a chiastic form of the chrismon, in a figure-ground relationship, where each capital is reflected by the same capital later in its horizontal line: "O . . . O" on the ends in line I, "M . . . M" in the penultimate places in line 2 and so forth. Note also the inversion on the alpha/omega pattern from first to last lines. Does the end to beginning equal beginning to end?

6d

```
            6    10    15    20    25    30    35
   FORTIA·FACTA·DVCIS·TOTO·DOMINANTIA·IAM·NVN        C
   ORBE·CANAM·QVIS·LAETA·S·VOS·VB·PRINCIPE·TANT      O
   RVRSVM·ROMA·TEN·ET·MVNDI·CAPVT·INCLITA·CVLME      N
   TV·VATEM·TV·DIVA·MONE·LACERATA·CRVENTI            S
 5 IMPERIIS·PARS·FESSA·POL·IDIVISA·GEMEBA            T
   SCEPTRA·ET·AVSO·NIAE·MAEREBAT·PERDITA·IVR         A
   SI·QVA·FIDES·TANTIS·ROMANVM·GLORIA·NOME           N
   INSIGNITTITVL·IS·DOMINOS·VT·LIBERA·QVAERAN        T
   MAESTAQVE·IVRE·SVOT·REPIDAT·PLAGA·MAXIMAMVND      I
10 VNDE·IVBAR·LVCIS·PRIMVM·RADIANS·HYPERIO           N
   SIDERIBVS·PVLS·IS·RVTILODIPFVNDITABORT            V
   INDE·TVVM·NOMEN·MVLTVM·MEMORABILE·CVNCTI          S
   MAXIME·BELLANT·VM·DOMITOR·LVX·VNICA·MVND          I
   PERPETVIS·VOTIS·CVPIVNT·VENERABILE·NVME           N
15 EXOPTANT·SERVI·RE·VOLVNT·MIRABILE·DICT            V
   REMQVE·LAREMQVE·ES·VVM·TANTA·EST·TIBI·GLORIA·IVST I
   AVGVSTO·IVVATE·CCET·VOS·VB·FOEDERE·IAM·NVN        C
   TOTVM·ORBEM·POST·TOT·CAEDES·QVAS·FESSA·GEMEBAN    T
   OMNIA·NVNC·NVLLO·TANDEM·TREPIDANTIA·MOT           V
20 ROMVLEIS·SERVI·REPIIS·PATER·INCLYTE·IVSSI         S
```

```
           5    10    15    20    25    30    35
   CONSTANTINE·PATER·TV·MVNDI·GLORIA·CONSVL
   EC·CET·VOR·EN·OVATA·DABIS·TOT·APERTA·LABORE
   REGNA·PER·INN·VMERAS·GENTES·MOX·CARVS·EOIS
   TOT·POP·VLIS·PIA·IVRA·FERES·ET·SOLVS·INOMNI
 5 AVGVST·VS·MVNDO·SPARGES·ET·IN·VLTIMA·NVMEN
   SOL·T·IBI·FELICES·FACIET·SPES·PERPETE·NVTV
   ARS·BONA·IVS·TITIAE·ET·DIVVM·VICINA·DECORI
   LARG·IDONA·BONI·CAE·LO·CAPIT·INFLVITILLVC
   VOTA·QVOD·OPTARINT·PIETATIS·CANAS·VBIVIT
10 SANCTA·CERES·TELLVS·REDDIT·BACHEIA·LAPSA
   RIVIS·DONAS·VIS·NON·EVRI·E·FLAMINE·TVRBANT
   ENORMES·PELAGVS·S·TATM·IT·IS·PRINCIPE·NOTO
   RES·PER·IVS·TA·VIGENS·ORIS·QVAS·IGNA·BOOTEN
   VLTIMA·CONSOCIAT·OLLVNT·INS·IDERA·DEXTRA
15 MAXIME·IVS·TITIAEL·VMEN·CONCORDIA·ET·OMEN
   PACIFIC·VM·TE·TOTA·CVP·IT·IAM·SAVC·IAE·TORAT
   RES·FESSA·S·CITO·PACE·LEVES·TV·IV·NGE·SEREN
   ORBIS·VOTA·TV·IGENTES·TIBI·IVNGE·VOLENTES
```

Two *versus intexti* of Optatian, honoring 'unconquerable Constantine.' In the first piece, the last word is stretched to fill the semantic space between its metrical completion and the final letter, contained in the third and final vertical column. This visual suspense will be later explored in the moiré compositions of Bernowin.

VITASALUSUIRTUSUERBUMSAPIENTIASPONSUS 7a
IANUAPASTOROUISPROLISQUEPARENTISIMAGO
RECTACOLUMNALAPISTURRISESLUCIFERETSOL
GRATIAPLENAPATRISAUGMENTUMLUCISABORTV
ALTITRONUSIESSUSLEXOPTIMAFACTOROLIMPI
CONSILIUMPRINCEPSREPLETUSFRUCTUSOLIUA
OMNIPOTENSUITISRECTORENUNCTORETUNCTUS
LEGIFERAETHERIUSTESTISDUXSERMOPROFETA
UICTORUBIQUETREMITTECAELIREGIAPRAESUL
MAXIMUSETMINIMUSSIGNUMUENERABILECULTU
BUTRUSESINCYPROMORSSERUUSUICTIMAMANNA
ARBITERAETERNUSNIMBVSQUOTERRAUIRESCAT
LAMPASESAUTPANISSVPERUSCOMMISUSABALTO
EXITUSINTROITUSSORSREGNUMSIUEREDEMTOR
ORBISESENMEDICUSPONENSPIGMENTASALUTIS
SIGNIFERINCLEPEISTUVINCISSEMPERETARCU
EMPTORADEPTUSERASCLARODESTIPITEMUNDUM
REXREGUMDOMINUSCUNCTISLUXALMAPERORBEM
PRINCIPIUMFINISLOCUPLESETPAUPERAMICTU
ENPUERETSENIORFONSFLUMENPASTORETAGNUS
NOMENHABENSORIENSVEXILLUMLUCISESORTUM
SIMPLICITERMITISMIRANDUSESOREPROFUSSO
FORTISSEUINFIRMUSTUPLENISSENSIBUSARON
IUSTUSESETIUDEXTUASOLUMSANCTAUOLUNTAS
REGNABEATATENENSDESTERCORESUMISEGENOS
MURUSESINUALIDISPVTEUSQUEMFEMINAPOTAT
IGNISINHUNCORBEMMISITQUEMUERUSABARCE
SUPREMUSQUEPARENSTRITUSTUPASSUSESABEL
SCRIBAESTUCERUUSCAPREADECESPITEBETHEL
INCLYTAPORTABONISPLANAETTUSEMITARECTA
MURSUSESINFERNIOREXCUIUSCELSATRIBUNAL
ASTRAPOLISUPERATPRIORACONSORTIBUSESTU
PACIFICUSSALOMONUERUSQUEOBLATUSESISAC
ENHOMOTUQUEDEUSPENSASQUIPROEMIACUIQUE
TUSTASDAMNANSOMNENEFASDEFENSORETULTOR
REXPIEUIRTUTUMTIBIGLORIAMYSTICESAMSON
AUXILIAREDECUSFLOSCAMPISUMMAQUEDEXTRA

Josephus Scotus: "On the names of Jesus for King Charles (Charlemagne)". An example of the conventional courtly *versus intexti,* closely imitated from Optatian, of the Carolingian period

b

De monogrammate, in quo Christi nomen comprehensum est.

ristusamorvotummiHiQuipiamuneradathaec
rminishicpretiūLIOViaPortiofidaqietis
ibonacunctaprobaNSOperantaettaliarite
nasuisfamulislargiturAdiSTaquecunctos
rtaturmiseransspoNDetpieCONditorarcem
npossimpetrarepOLifceptRAaltaqeregna
spesfirmafidessumMIetcupIthiCEAfancte
stusamornecamatmemoransha ecpERDit:orsa
naqidemhaecvenieNsHucorbeMLiTelucunda
arseratinmundoantEriorevALentiafructu
odocuitmundumdediCaNseinDEteriorahic
accepsmalletabirelocAdAnaiuramagister
scereuangeliietdIRumManssescermorem
deusarcepolietiuScuscumadueneritistuc
clorabaethereiiufTIsdaropraemiapatris
xtratuncmeritiscapiatbeamuneradignis
tequidemnumerusfaNantissignatvtrumque
ventumdominihincArCebatquandotyrannum
andovIRHicfactaStanTbonareddiDitorbi
stq;eSuumGunctisbAptiImaprobaEdiditore
csumMOESTquandofa.LnamapatreiuSTiturus
dexeTbomOfaLPixiStUmprOeMiasanctahinc
rtpriUSHisAltodAreeTVfQEVideresuperni
mpesacramfaCIemquosverUSNnntiatauetus
sebonismeritisypfAILendumcanticapartos
aecantaresoletfoRSAlmavtforiptaserena
ocalypsishabentdILUcidaibiagminaferre
oriavirtusecCfeoltoomneniEatqeperaeuum
leluiasonatQuisoHTAmenaUIaerithaudhac
deusetdominUsplAcanDusNoStervbiqueest
odiuuETisnosforIPTIOvtalmeftAErisarce
appaRebitouansfEruoRumhincetRaPitalmi
rbaniHIlperdensaCSCandalainaBMouetira
uotosfamulosfrumentavtmittatInhorreum
lixquivaletatqelíCetcuiscanderecaelum
lactumdominibenecriftiintenderevultum
imanetaltusamorpeRlectioreddituromnis
gelicisquechorispermxtusgaudetvbique
udibusetcertatcanTando,sallerechristo
nticaritenouahocStUdiumeeponernesceit
gnaquiaaeternaIlctuMetbenegaudianouit

Rabanus Maurus: "The monogram, wherein the name of Christ is contained." Monogram and *versus intexti* combine, as do Latin and Greek, in this piece. The horizontal text is in Latin, the vertical, which is also the monogram composed of all the letters needed to form the words "Jesus Christ Son of God," is Greek. The poet also used different colored inks to fill out the design, giving this poem a very tapestry-like quality. The weakening of the straightness and patternedness of the vertical, 'imperial' text marks this as a late—ninth century—composition. Note that the Greek letters form a chrismon.

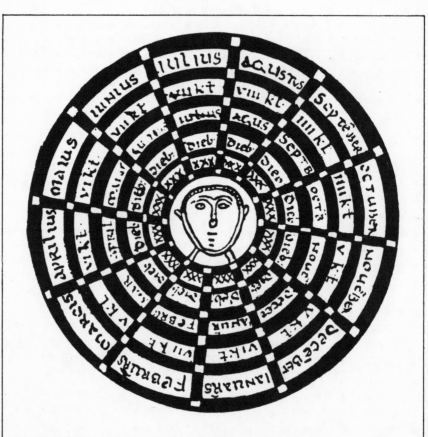

A calendar in the form of the cosmos. Earth is represented by the human face. Rings correspond to days, months, etc. From the seventh-century scholar, Isidore of Seville.

7c   PRÆFATIO.

Musacitastudiogaudensnuncdicerenumen
Nostracupitparitercarmineetalloquiis
Donapatrissummiqaelargusreddiditorbi
Regisetaltithronisanctatrophaeasimul
Quaecruxestsacracrucifixinumineplena
Omnibusaptabonisstirpsvenerandasatis
Hancegopauperegenusinopsenoreloqella
Temptauihicfamuilussonsdarecthocoriar
Necmefactapiantquoddignummuneretanto
Meforeadhocceredamsicquoqementeprobum
Sedmihilargadeibonitasspesmaximavoti
Estquaemepromptumlausdabatexhilarans
Pauperisetviduaenonspreuitraraminuta
Sedtulitipsaprobansarbiteromnitenens
Atqueorbedominansqisancitsolusetvnus
Cunctavenustibonahanclaudebeauiiamor
Mandatumvetirenempeestetlegequibusqe
Munerautap.adarenttemplaadhonestadei
Parsdedit.rgentumparsaurimuneraclara
Parstrib'itgemmasparsqoqetinctadedit
Lignaoleumqidampigmentaqueearadedere
Multaq;ragnadomusmonstratvbiqnemicans
Astaliisetastulerantpilosquecaprarum
Necfuerantspretihidonaferendodeohaec
Quapropterrogitonummatumdiuesvtistic
Viliacumportemhiucspernerenollitonus
Ipselicetgazasinmensasconferatamplis
Agminibusfultustemplaonerandadeihinc
Hisegononmotusconturbornamimpievultu
Sedgratulansspeculorcresceredonasibi
Illequoqueexosavthabeatmeamuneranolo
Sedmagisessesciatqualiacumquedeihaec
Exprobratipsedeoqidespicitaceregenum
Cuiusegenushicestcuiusetomnishomoest
Etqantumtribuotribuitmihiiesusamator
Sintsuafactapiehiccunctaquehicrapiat

Rabanus Maurus: "Preface." Actually an invocation to the Christian muse, the Holy Ghost. Here, the inwoven text is scattered into an apparently random series of emphasized letters which, when assembled, read: *Magnentius Hrabanus Maurus hoc opus fecit* ("Magnentius Hrabanus Maurus 'made'[*facere*] this work."). The result is the vertical text has just about lost all its in-forming influence on the pattern.

The moiré poem of Bernowin   8

```
DetChristus Dominator enim  De semine   D    a   v   i   D
Eternam Exiguo vitam da     Eternus     E t     i p s E
Vitalis Vita    et          Victor      Victoria    IesV
Sempiterne Simul            Semper tu   Solus es almuS
Mitis tu Miserere mei et    Miserere    M   e   o   r u M
Iustus tu Iudex             Iusta et    Iudicia   servI
Sola salus Spes             Sola fiducia Semper  et aptuS
Excelsus  Excelsa  petens   Excelsus    E t     i p s E
Rem repara Retributor       Rex pius atque RedemptoR
Ecclesiae Ecclesiarum auctor bonus Emptor E t   i p s E
Rex regum Regnans           Regnorum    Rector amatoR
Erue tu Exiguum             Eripe egenum Egentem et ubiquE
```

9a   PYRAMIDA AD LEONEM IMPERATOREM

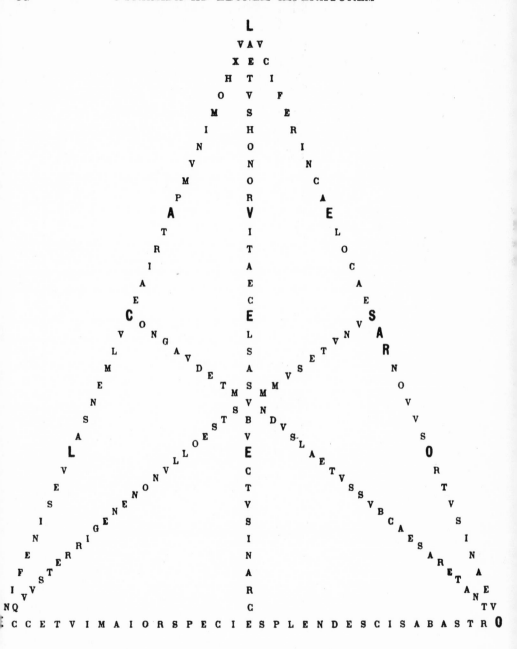

An 'unfinished' poem of Eugenius Vulgarius, where the square has been suppressed into a triangle. Late example, but typical dedicatory situation of the *versus intexti.*

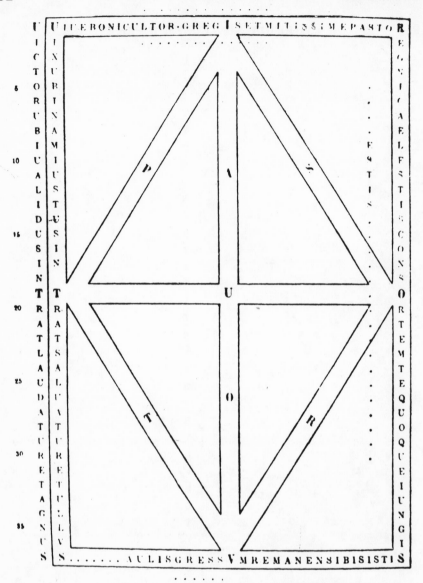

Another example of a late *versus intexti,* this is from the monastery of San Gallo. Here, practically all text has been swept away, except for standard phrases praising the emperor, which are not integrated into the metrical, mathematical, or spatial patterns of the form. Rather, they seem to exist outside the design, as borders, comments, labels, and sometimes, explanations (e.g., the last line—"to the splendor and health of king and court"). (*Note:* the dots indicate illegible or partly erased letters.)

ON LANGUAGE AND VISUAL LANGUAGE

Loris Essary

We are obsessed by but not possessed of an algorithmic language.

Assumptions:

- that poem is most complete when it unequivocally points to objects, ideas, events, relations; leaves nothing more to be desired; contains nothing which it does not reveal; and thereby drives us toward the object which it designates.

- that it is composed from a universal language which possesses in advance anything it may wish to express, because its elements, words and syntax mirror the fundamental possibilities and their articulations.

- of its own, a word holds no virtue, but is a pure sign standing for pure signification.

- the poet is encoding his thoughts, replacing his thoughts with a pattern we may hear or see.

- thought understanding itself is self-sufficient; the thoughts signify nothing beyond themselves and are conveyed to other minds which understand them because they attach the same signification to the same sign whether out of habit, convention, or even divine intention.

- "We never find among other people's words that we have not put there." —Maurice Merleau-Ponty.

Taken individually, however, signs do not signify anything. Each discrete sign does not express a single meaning as much as it denotes a difference of meaning between other signs and itself, opposites, relations, affirmations, negations. Since this is the case of all other signs, language is made up of differences without terms. More precisely, the terms of language are generated only by the differences among them. "Whether one takes the signified or the signifying, language contains neither ideas nor sounds that could pre-exist before the linguistic system, but only conceptual differences and phonic differences which result from this system." —Ferdinand de Saussure.

> The apparition of these faces in the crowd:
> Petals on a wet, black bough.
> —Ezra Pound.

— Does Pound signify your face or mine?
— What if you have never seen my face?
— Does he intend to signify only those faces one would reasonably
    expect to see in the Paris underground? (I have never been
    to France.)
— Of what plant are the 'petals' appendages?
— At what point does dampness become 'wetness'?
— How large must a branch be before we perceive it as a 'bough'?
— Is there a maximum limit of size at which point it ceases to be a
    'bough' and becomes something else? If so, at which particu-
    lar point in between is this particular object?

So: *what does Pound's poem mean?*

There is a story told of how Matisse was filmed in slow motion as he
worked at his canvas. The naked eye perceived a deliberate, continual
application of paint to achieve a specific intention of form and color.
The film revealed, however, that the same brush which, to the eye,
did not jump from one moment to the next, could be seen beginning
ten possible movements, dancing almost touching the painting several
times, and finally dropping into the only stroke necessary. "In his
mind's eye, he did not have all the possible gestures, he did not have
to eliminate all but one of them to make his choice rational." The particular stroke was selected in order to satisfy ten conditions scattered
on the canvas "unformulated and unformulable for anyone other than
Matisse, since they were defined and imposed only by the intention to
make *this particular painting which did not yet exist.*" What is true
of Matisse is also true of language. "Speech does not choose only
one sign for one already defined signification the way one searches for
a hammer to drive in a nail or pincers to pull one out....It gropes
around an intention to signify which has no text to guide it, for it is
just being written. And if we want to grasp speech in its most authen-
tic operation in order to do it full justice, we must evoke all those
words that could have come in its place that have been omitted; to
feel the different way they would have impinged on and rattled the
chain of language, to know at what point this particular speech was
the only one possible." Or, put another way, "One does not know
what one is saying, one knows after one has said it." —Merleau-Ponty.

A poem is always in a state of being, never an accurate representation
of the world or an exhaustive inventory of the possibilities of experi-

ence. It is the language of the poem in its incompleteness that invites us to take up the poet's gesture and complete it, to go beyond disparate signs to *a signification of the possible.* The more closely a poet works to exactly reproduce emotions, objects, *a thing,* the further away he is from them. His language has reproduced not the world and what is involved in the world but a mimesis of stasis.

The Second Law of Thermodynamics: all systems fall apart, no structure is possible and, finally, there is death. What is true of thermodynamics in which entropy is a measure of disorganization is not true of language. "The information carried by a set of messages is a measure of organization."—Norbert Wiener. "That information should be measured by entropy...is natural when we remember that information is associated with the amount of freedom of choice we have in constructing messages. Thus one can say of a communication source... 'this situation is highly organized; it is not characterized by a large degree of randomness or of choice—that is to say, the information or the entropy is low'....The word information relates not so much to what you *do* say, as to what you *could* say. That is, information is a measure of your freedom of choice, when you select a message.... The greater this freedom of choice, the greater is the uncertainty that the message actually selected is some particular one. Thus greater freedom of choice, greater uncertainty and greater information all go hand in hand." —Warren Weaver.

Before language, before Pound's poem, we are all like a child for whom a single word is a sentence and even phonemes words. As we examine each word—'apparition,' 'of,' 'faces,' 'the,' 'crowd',—testing each against all possible cases of itself, new associations are generated, combinations formed which have not formed before. Whether we are able to reproduce the poet's particular signification or not, our own signification has grown, mutated into something new. *We are more than we were.* Rather than enslaved to a determinant world, we have been liberated from it, and, once free, we return to it as its creator. A complete work, observed Baudelaire, is not necessarily finished, and a finished work is not necessarily complete. The idea of *complete* expression is the only nonsense. Merleau-Ponty: "If we rid our minds of the idea that language is the translation or cipher of an original text, we should see that ...all language is indirect or allusive—that it is, if you wish, silence."

Language is as much an aspect of our physical self as it is our minds. The 'imprinting' by which we internalize a grammar and the necessary rules of transformation assume a neurochemical or neurophysical basis in our bodies themselves. Studies of the speech defect aphasia show clearly the direct and specific relations between physiology and language. Any statement accompanied by a common blush adds an additional sign to the total set of signs and alters our perception of its final signification. As with words themselves, there is considerable possibility for the maximization of information within this physical aspect of language. The simple blush is no less equivocal than Pound's faces. According to the context it may indicate pleasure or shame. Or anger or passion. As we visualize (physicalize) language, we can more wholly explore the possibilities of what we have to say.

Traditional typography assumes a limited interest in the spatial importance of language. Words that a poet desires to emphasize may be entirely capitalized, or emphasis may be achieved by the use of multiple exclamation points. A line stop may occur in the middle of a word, breaking it into two syllables, each with a meaning different from that of a word were it printed as a whole. Unintentionally, even printers' conventions can change the visual perception of a word or an entire poem. Whether a punctuation mark is joined to or separated from a word by a quotation mark alters the possible signification of the physical event when considered in and of itself and not understood through an appeal to the standardization of grammar. A word or words appearing at the end of a long and unmanageable sentence suddenly appear(s) indented on the right as a separate line, struck off from the rest of the text by a bracket. To the left, a spatial break in the text has occurred, creating a visually significant space where none was intended in the manuscript.

Visual poetry maximizes physical signification. An exclamation point always signifies an exclamation. A shift in type size within and throughout a word indicates only an *intensity*. Size can open up the chronology of a poetic event. Given no perceptible determinant sequence of arrangement, the reader of a visual poem, instead of being forced into a conventional sequence of left-to-right, top-to-bottom across a page, may select his own entrance to the page, scanning the notation of one size of characters, going on to another as *his* sense dictates. Arrows, which are not usually assumed to be linguistic indicators, may be introduced to create vectors of potential meaning. They are capable of leading readers back to spatial areas of a poem without forcing the repetitious printing of the exact text that delimits that area. We cannot step in the same river twice, or return to a notation unmodified by what has come temporally and spatially later in the poem as well as in our own language inventory. The possibilities of a single word are at least as broad as the number of type faces in which it may be reproduced. The word 'how' signifies one thing in sans serif, another in serifs. Or within the sans-serif family itself, certain possible meanings are signified in helvetica face, others affirmed and denied in cairoli.

New 'words' are also possible, not so much neologisms which assume their place within the meanings of language as we already have it, but new signification at the phoneme level. As with language as a whole, they constitute a system, are less a limited number of tools than a representative way of modulation, with a limitless potential for differentiating one gesture of our language from another. Suppose the meaning we wish to create is exactly signified by the conjoining of the letters 'b' and 'l'. Were we simply to indicate that by a spatial separation within a group of syllables and phonemes, the reader would follow his habit of combining all familiar elements into a word he has already assimilated and thereby aborting the new possibility we have to share. Reproduced in a unique typeface which reflects in its size and form the signification to be found in it, it is possible to establish even the independence of phonemes, as well as the independence of their signification. Made visually systematic, the internal order of the process becomes a suggestion, not that there is no meaning, not that this is an 'experiment,' but that we must again become the child who is just learning to speak about a world he is just learning to discover.

That child stands before the structure of a new alphabet. We do not frequently recall that the most elemental structures of our language began from this juncture of the physical, visual and sonorous. The letter 'k', which the Phoenicians called *kaph,* meant to them the palm of a hand'and the letter was drawn to represent this juncture. The letter 'l', which they pronounced *lamed,* was drawn to resemble a crooked staff or possibly a gourd, or even the rod of a teacher. The letter 'j' only evolved from the letter 'i' in the seventeenth century when it was perceived that an initial 'i' sound was almost always that of a consonant. When two 'i's' appeared consecutively, printers began to add a curved tail to the second in order to differentiate it from the first. Through the accidents to which language is always susceptible, the signs for the sounds were reversed when standardization occurred. Notation and the sense data it notates are not inevitably linked, immune to evolution. As our central nervous systems continue to be externalized beyond our bodies, as *we ourselves become media,* no rigid system of notation can ever expect to communicate more than a fraction of our messages.

It may be argued that we have moved beyond poetry and into an art
not unlike drawing or painting. Brackets, arrows, shafts are not linguistic notations in the accepted sense that we understand our speech
to operate. Yet there is no analysis of grammar that can demonstrate
elements common to all languages. One language does not necessarily
contain the modes of expression found in another. The African language Peul signifies the negative by intonation alone. Particles exist
in Greek which are untranslatable in Greek itself. Pronouns such as
'I,' 'you,' 'me,' 'it' which begin as words almost always appear joined
to their verbs, as in 'I write,' and may be treated as a type of frontal
inflection of the verb itself, almost becoming semantemes. They are
analogous to the verbs in Latin which take their person from an ending which has become an inseparable part of the verb itself. *Scribo.* I
write. "A morphological system always contains only a restricted
number of categories which impose themselves and are dominant.
But in each system there are always other categories in the process of
disappearing or, on the contrary, of taking shape." —Joseph Vendryès.
We are dealing here not so much with words as with "coefficients,"
"exponents," or "linguistic tools," which have use value rather than
signification. Brackets. Arrows. Shafts. Each has no signifying power that we can isolate, but, when joined together in a verbal chain,
make unquestionable sense. Were more visual poets to read their
work aloud, this sense would be apparent. Consider my "Poem at Pt.
Reyes." Read it aloud as a simple list of objects, enumerate the
squares, numbers and arrows. Read it a second time using the arrows
as pitch indicators for intonation. Read it a third time, adding to the
techniques of the first readings an emotional 'feel' for the poem based
on ink density, whether a shape is substantially open or closed. Then:
define a 'mountain.' Speak the word 'mountain.' In German. In
French. In Persian. Feel a 'mountain.' In German. In French. In
Persian. What *is* a mountain? Or the sea? If you tell someone all you
know of a 'mountain,' in German, in French, in Persian, does he
know what a mountain *is?*

At the root of all visual poetry is the question of our freedom. If we
desire to be free to experience that out of which we build our poems,
can we desire the freedom of those who read our poems any less than
our own? Are we so certain of our own absolute perception of reality
that we have ossified past that point at which we are willing to learn
from and be more than we were because of the expansion and recre-
ation of our work in another? Unless our language is as much beyond
us as in us, we should never speak at all and be only what we were,
never what we are. "Each different tongue," George Steiner observes,
"offers its own denial of determinism. 'The world,' it says, 'can be
other.' Ambiguity, polysemy, opaqueness, the violation of grammat-

ical and logical sequences, reciprocal incomprehensions, the capacity to lie—these are not pathologies of language but the roots of its genius."

(for Merleau-Ponty, whose work, particularly *The Prose of the World* and *Signs,* is central to the issues we encounter in language, both non-visual and visual)

a
B

)VALIO-

such

sea

BRITTLE

peeled

[film]

odd
_____

NE

7

MISC

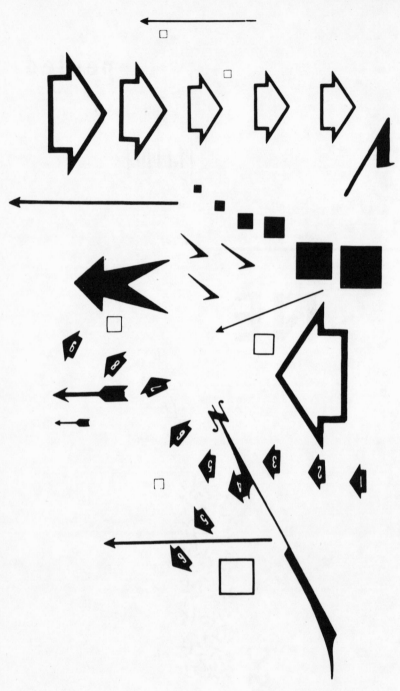

POEM AT PT. REYES

THE I CHING AS VISUAL POEM

Jonathan Price

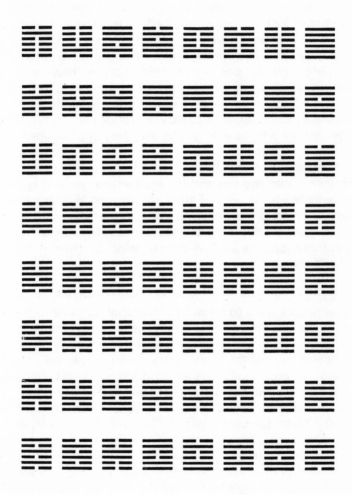

Want to know the future? First you bake a turtle. If its belly pops open, the answer is "bad luck." If the lines go all the way across, the answer is "good fortune." That simple ritual brought answers to Chinese peasants five thousand years ago, asking questions of the priestesses of Mother Earth.

These forms, so simple, so orderly, have intrigued people for over five thousand years, and what these people have said about them has

gradually accumulated in the thick commentaries that accompany the
lines. One scholar suggests that you read all the judgments when you
first cast your fortune; then, having absorbed the verbal meaning, you
may recall the gist of it simply by looking the the pictures.

In this sense, the *I Ching* may be seen as a visual poem, with extensive footnotes for each line. In their various visual forms, the hexagrams are supposed to represent everything that can happen to you.
Seen from another perspective, the *I Ching* is a systemic work, in
which specific meanings have been attached to each of 64 numbers by
methodical application of certain rules. A primitive Chinese writer in-
terprets these permutations as all the situations we may face; a computer expert recognizes the binary code for numbers 0 to 63 here.
Reading the *I Ching* then is a performance involving the fortune teller,
the questioner, and a series of chance operations which produce visible forms, which a fortune teller can interpret in whispered suggestions.

The interpretations, though, are not arbitrary, but systematic. The
basic forms are the long line and the broken line: yes and no, male and
female, positive and negative, Father Heaven and Mother Earth. Such
rudimentary readings represent the most ancient level of this archeo-
logical dig. Over time, the priestesses seem to have noticed that you
could get more sophisticated answers by analyzing these lines in combinations of three:

Each trigram, or three-line figure, it was decided, could stand for
key things people want to know: so each trigram came to be associated with a certain time of year or day, geographical location, animal,
kitchen utensil, farm tool, plant, member of the family, type of
weather, color, part of the body, disease, sign of the zodiac, mood,
and style of action. Thus, depending on the question being asked of
the priestess, the same trigram might mean: winter afternoon, south-
west, mare, cauldron, wagon, yellow flowers, mother, cloudy days,
black, belly, birth, Cancer in part of Leo, receptive, fertile, and yield-
ing.

Naturally, people began to combine these three-line figures in as
many different permutations as they could work out, producing a
total of sixty-four hexagrams (six line figures). These, they said, represent all the possibilities of life. Their titles alone suggest the
breadth of advice and analysis: the creative, the receptive, difficult
beginning, young fool, waiting, conflict, the army, holding together,
the taming power of the small, treading lightly, peace, standstill, fel-
lowship, vast possession, modesty, enthusiasm, following, work on
what has been spoiled, approach, contemplation, biting through,
grace, splitting apart, the turning point, innocence, the taming power of the great, providing nourishment, preponderance of the great,

abyss, clinging fire, wooing, long-lasting, retreat, the power of the
great, progress, darkening light, the family, opposition, obstruction,
deliverance, decrease, increase, break-through, coming to meet, gathering together, pushing upward, exhaustion, the well, revolution,
cauldron, thunderous shock, keeping still, gradual progress, marry-
ing maiden, abundance, the wanderer, gentle wind, joyous lake, dis-
persion, limitation, inner truth, preponderance of the small, after
completion, before completion.

The six slots became identified with positions on the body (the
lowest represents the feet and ankles, the highest is the head), status
in the state (the top is the wise sage, who has retired from the world;
the next to the top is the emperor), stages of an action (the bottom
is the preliminaries, the next line the true beginning, the top has
passed beyond caring). Certain slots, then, ought to be soft, others
hard, some strong, others deferential; some male, others female.
Hence, if you got a female (broken) line where a male should be expected, you could count on trouble. Further refinement came when
people spotted 'nuclear' trigrams hidden inside the hexagram, and announced that these too influenced the changing pattern of events.
And, with the new chance operations for finding the hexagrams (by
heads or tails with coins, or by a complex tossing-out of yarrow
stalks), the questioner sometimes came up with three heads, a line
that had gone so far one way the Chinese knew it was bound to turn
into its opposite in a little while. These changing lines do turn into
their opposites, to provide you with a second hexagram, and more advice.

So with all these associations for trigrams just under the visual surface, the hexagrams offer any fortune-teller a wealth of things to say,
even when he does not know what question the client holds closest
to the heart. Much of the interpretation comes in symbolic forms
borrowed from nature: thunder, lakes, rivers, wind, mountains, ocean,
fire, heaven and earth. And we get the raw data for a dream, too: an
animal, a color, a time, weather, a place, certain characters, acts, and
a tone.

What seems to happen during a reading is this: the client has to collect himself, figuring out the most important questions he has. This
alone helps him begin to answer it. Usually he has two opposing answers: one that he wants to do, another that he thinks he ought to do.
In Freudian terms, the impulses of the id have run flat into the restric-
tive morals of the superego: what to do? Ask King Wen, the man who
wrote down the first set of interpretations.

When King Wen talks, he talks in images. Not riddles, like Greek
prophetesses at Dodona. Natural symbols. And the listener's mind,
already calmed by resolving on a query, and by tossing the coins in
submission to chance, responds to these images by reading meaning

into them. Often, as the fortune-teller talks, the listener exclaims, "Oh!" Muscles relax. Breath expands. The eyes brighten. The backbone straightens.

That discovery resembles the moment in therapy when the patient finds out what he really wants. As with a more conventional poem, we project our deeper intentions onto the poet; we find our real feelings expressed, and we thank the poet for having articulated our innermost thoughts. Is this psychic? Perhaps; but surely it is human.

Such a verbo-visual system seems simultaneously contemporary and primitive because its purpose is not the expression of King Wen's private agony, but the ritual of self-discovery for the reader. The experience, then, seems to change the state of consciousness of the listener, giving him access to parts of his mind he does not use in everyday life. Intuition, or high mind—whatever name we give these states—we recognize their depth, and their antiquity.

A HOMAGE AND AN ALPHABET
Two Recent Works by Ian Hamilton Finlay

Stephen Scobie

Over ten years ago, Ian Hamilton Finlay published a series of what he called "One Word Poems." His method was to use the title to indicate an area of metaphor, and then to insert a single word, the name of an object, as the true "poem." Whereas another poet might name a poem, for instance, "Swallow," and then present, as the text of the poem, a series of metaphors on swallows, Finlay relegated the metaphoric activity to the title, insisting that the beauty lies in the natural object itself, not in the fancy ideas we weave around it. Thus:

THE CLOUD'S ANCHOR

swallow

As Finlay's poetry has developed, over the years, into what must I suppose be called his post-concrete phase, the relationship between text and title has, in many of his works, become even more subtle and complex. The purpose of this essay is to examine two works— "Homage to Watteau" (Wild Hawthorn Press, 1975) and "The Boy's Alphabet Book" (Coach House Press, 1977)—in which the apparent "text" is very simple, indeed minimal, and in which the poetic activity goes on largely in the context set up by the title and by the form of presentation.

I

The reading of any poem depends upon the interaction between the text and the sets of conventional expectations which the reader brings to bear upon it. No one reads a poem literally: even the simplest metaphor brings into play a complex range of responses about what a metaphor is, what kind of reality it has in relation to other kinds of reality, modes and limits of interpretation, etc. The simple assertion of *being a poem* gives to any text a context which in many ways determines how it is to be read.

In many of Finlay's works, the poetic activity consists largely of establishing such a context, the "field" (sometimes literally) of "being a poem." Within this field, one concise image—often reduced to a single proper name, number, or fact—can extend its significance in a witty and controlled play among the levels evoked by the context. In such minimal art, as the *range* of choice narrows (for both poet and reader), so the *quality* of choice becomes more important, for it is only within the most rigorous limits that the assertion of "being a poem" can be maintained and validated.

In Finlay's "Homage to Watteau," the relation of context to text is quite literally realized as a surround, a folder. As in Finlay's earlier Watteau poem, "Cythera," where the rhythm of reading was determined by the physical action of turning the pages of a pamphlet or of walking through a garden, the physical form of the poem's presentation is an *enactment* of metaphoric relations which the "conventional" poem would indicate through discursive syntax. The folder proclaims title, sub-title, author, and press; inside, the "text" consists of a single sheet of fine quality paper, in a delicate blue-green shade, and its identifying trade-name, "Antique Wove."

This text is in itself beautiful—especially as the words, while still retaining their technical status as trade-name, are also freed to pursue the rich associations of their original meanings—but it only becomes a *poem* in relation to the context established by the folder. It is the context which controls the range of associations, otherwise random, and "weaves" them into a "homage."

Firstly, and principally, the complete ensemble of the "title page" initiates the assertion that *this is a poem,* and thus demands a certain kind of attention, or way of reading. The reader may expect a concise, carefully fashioned structure, which has fully articulated all the necessary pre-conditions for significance—a significance which will probably be realized through metaphoric or imagistic activity.

Secondly, the main title: "Homage to Watteau." The word "Homage" indicates the genre, thus narrowing and specifying the reader's expectations. It places the poem within a tradition: a tradition which is itself intensely conscious of tradition, and of continuity. In a "homage," one artist brings his own sensibility to bear upon another's; the result is a statement about each artist individually, and also about the way they relate to each other within the continuity of culture. Because, for Finlay, culture *is* a continuity: there is no decisive barrier between himself, as a poet writing in a contemporary, post-Concrete idiom, and Jean-Antoine Watteau (1684-1721). The title may also serve to place the poem alongside Finlay's own other "Homages," which have been to painters as diverse as Malevich and Vuillard, as well as to the critic and art dealer, Daniel-Henry Kahnweiler.

The sub-title specifies which particular Watteau painting Finlay has in mind—"L'Embarquement pour Cythère"—and also brings into play the associations of Finlay's own earlier poem, "Cythera," written some ten years before. This lyric introduced one of the central "puns" (it would be better, perhaps, if more pedantic, to call them *word transformations*) in Finlay's work: the metamorphosis of "bark" into "barque," tree into boat, land into sea, natural phenomenon into cultural artifact. The metaphoric identification of diverse elements is Finlay's central technique, and theme.

Finally, the author's name, and the name of his press, relate this particular work to the complete range of Finlay's production: both to its themes (the continuity of culture, the metaphorical identity of the elements) and to its tradition of craftsmanship, the care and attention to detail that go into all Wild Hawthorn Press publications.

Within this context, it may now be possible to suggest at least some of the various ways in which the text can be "read." Thus, "antique" may be taken to refer to the distance of age which separates us from the historical time of Watteau, from the mythological time of Cythera (birthplace of Aphrodite), or even, alas, from the craftsman's time of fine paper. The ideas of age are reinforced by the past tense of "wove," which also suggests a tapestry in which various levels are woven together, just as Watteau's painting of a classical scene inhabited by figures in 18th century dress weaves together the mythological past and the cultural standards of his own time. The paper itself can also carry connotations: its color reflects the colors of both Watteau's painting and the earlier Finlay poem; and one could go so far as to remark that one of the original materials of paper is bark— but bark metamorphosed, as in Finlay's poem, into something subtler and lovelier. The paper is also the product of a *craftsman,* whose love and care for his craft is as precious, as rare, and as central to the continuity of culture, as that of the artist—Watteau, or Finlay.

II

In *The Boy's Alphabet Book,* the "text" is again very simple. It consists of brief, factual descriptions of the objects exemplifying each letter of the alphabet, from A for Amphibian airplane to Z for Scottish Zulu fishing luggers. The language of this text carefully avoids any "poetic" elaborations. There are only a couple of similes—"Battle fleets are like families," "Xmas trees. . .look a little like moon-rockets"—both suggested by the accompanying photographs. The metaphoric interplay of elements is hinted at in "Amphibian"—"It can take off (or land) on land or on the sea"—and in "Flattop"—"A flattop is a floating landing-field." But for the most part the text amounts to no more than simple identifications: "Drifters and trawlers are two kinds of fishing boats which catch sea-fish with nets."

Stephen Bann has referred to Finlay's use of "every variety of pre-constrained linguistic formula—cliché, proverb, riddle, headline, title, registration sign" as a way "to emphasize [language's] public character, its status as the common change of everyday communication, whilst simultaneously conferring upon it a private, poetic meaning" (Serpentine Gallery Catalogue, 1977). The deliberately simplified use of language suitable for a child's ABC is just such a pre-constrained formula. By its very simplicity, it draws the reader's attention to problems of definition. "When a sailor means 'behind' he says

'abaft.' '' The process of signification is always a complex interaction
of many variables, of which the straightforward denotative meaning
of words is only one. In this book, the language's very refusal to be
metaphorical draws attention to itself, causing the reader to question
the adequacy of the definitions provided by the verbal text. As in the
"Homage to Watteau," what has happened is that the metaphoric or
poetic activity has been displaced from the ostensible "text," and is
to be found in the whole form surrounding and presenting the text.

And again, the title is the first basic indication. *The Boy's Alphabet Book.* (Is any special significance to be read into the singular
"boy's"? I don't think so, unless it is to be taken as a personal reference to Finlay's own son.) The title suggests an entirely traditional
form: like a "homage," it sets itself within a continuity, of primers,
of "First Readers" (like Gertrude Stein's), of alphabet poems, of the
fascination which concrete poets have always felt for illustrated al-
phabets and pictorial letters (the kind of thing so extensively collected by Massin in *La Lettre et L'Image,* Gallimard 1970.)

Indeed, it is so traditional that it is almost reactionary. In this age
of non-sexist children's literature, to limit a book about ships and
planes and kites and gliders to boys only is to make a gesture as consciously anachronistic as to celebrate *war*ships and *war*planes in an
age of liberal anti-militarism. This comment may strike Finlay himself as odd—in his own household, his daughter Ailie is as fully involved in the world of *The Boy's Alphabet Book* as is his son Eck—
but the title does set up a context which stands slightly aside from
the urbanized world of the late 1970s, just as Finlay himself has chosen to live "slightly aside from" the city of Edinburgh.

Another context for the book is, as with the "homage to Watteau,"
that of Finlay's own previous work. The range of subject-matter,
from fishing-boats to aircraft carriers, is familiar territory, and the
book reads like a series of footnotes to the icons of Finlay's imagination. L for Lugger explains what a stay-sail is; one of the stone carv-
ings in *Selected Ponds* has "Stay-Sail" as its text. I for Inshore fishing
vessel mentions a seine-net, and one is reminded of "Purse-Net Boat":

                              seiner
                       seiner
               seiner   silver
                       seiner
                          seiner

(The association is reinforced by the accompanying photograph, in
which the sea is represented by crushed silver paper.) Just as an alpha-
bet-book teaches children how to read, so Finlay's book teaches us
how to read his poems.

Then there is the fact that the objects mentioned are represented
in the book not by themselves but by carved wooden toys, small-scale

models. (Some of them are working models: J illustrates a simple
jet engine, and paternally warns "Do not try this by yourself!")
Again, the fact that these are home-made toys, models carved by
Finlay himself for his own children, serves to set the book aside from
the contemporary world of mass-produced toys, Muppet puppets and
Sesame Street dolls, which standardize and homogenize the imagina-
tions of whole generations. The toys in this book represent a tradition of craftsmanship which, like that of the papermaker of "Antique
Wove," is in danger of becoming not merely anachronistic but extinct.
     The function of small-scale models in Finlay's work has been wide-
ly commented on; Stephen Bann especially has evoked the ideas of
Claude Lévi-Strauss, and it will be sufficient here to recall a key passage from *The Savage Mind:*

> Now, the question arises whether the small-scale model or miniature,
> which is also the 'masterpiece' of the journeyman may not in fact be the
> universal type of the work of art. All miniatures seem to have intrinsic aes-
> thetic quality—and from what should they draw this constant virtue if not
> from the dimensions themselves?—and conversely the vast majority of
> works of art are small-scale. It might be thought that this characteristic is
> principally a matter of economy in materials and means, and one might ap-
> peal in support of this theory to works which are incontestably artistic but
> also on a grand scale. We have to be clear about definitions. The paintings
> of the Sistine Chapel are a small-scale model in spite of their imposing di-
> mensions, since the theme which they depict is the End of Time. The same
> is true of the cosmic symbolism of religious monuments. Further, we may
> ask whether the aesthetic effect, say, of an equestrian statue which is larger
> than life derives from its enlargement of a man to the size of a rock or
> whether it is not rather due to the fact that it restores what is at first from
> a distance seen as a rock to the proportions of a man. Finally even 'natur-
> al size' implies a reduction of scale since graphic or plastic transposition
> always involves giving up certain dimensions of the object: volume in paint-
> ing, color, smell, tactile impressions in sculpture and the temporal dimen-
> sion in both cases since the whole work represented is apprehended at a sin-
> gle moment in time.
>   What is the virtue of reduction either of scale or in the number of prop-
> erties? It seems to result from a sort of reversal in the process of under-
> standing. To understand a real object in its totality we always tend to
> work from its parts. The resistance it offers us is overcome by dividing it.
> Reduction in scale reverses this situation. Being smaller, the object as a
> whole seems less formidable. By being quantitatively diminished, it seems
> to us qualitatively simplified. More exactly, this quantitative transposition
> extends and diversifies our power over a homologue of the thing, and by
> means of it the latter can be grasped, assessed and apprehended at a glance.
> A child's doll is no longer an enemy, a rival or even an interlocutor. In it
> and through it a person is made into a subject. In the case of miniatures, in
> contrast to what happens when we try to understand an object or living
> creature of real dimensions, knowledge of the whole precedes knowledge
> of the parts. And even if this is an illusion, the point of the procedure is to
> create or sustain the illusion, which gratifies the intelligence and gives rise
> to a sense of pleasure which can already be called aesthetic on these grounds
> alone.

I have so far only considered matters of scale which, as we have just seen, imply a dialectical relation between size (i.e. quantity) and quality. But miniatures have a further feature. They are 'man made' and, what is more, made by hand. They are therefore not just projections or passive homologues of the object: they constitute a real experiment with it. Now the model being an artifact, it is possible to understand how it is made and this understanding of the method of construction adds a supplementary dimension. As we have already seen in the case of 'bricolage,' and the example of 'styles' of painters shows that the same is true in art, there are several solutions to the same problem. The choice of one solution involves a modification of the result to which another solution would have led, and the observer is in effect presented with the general picture of these permutations at the same time as the particular solution is offered. He is thereby transformed into an active participant without even being aware of it. Merely by contemplating it he is, as it were, put in possession of other possible forms of the same work; and in a confused way, he feels himself to be their creator with more right than the creator himself because the latter abandoned them in excluding them from his creation. And these forms are so many further perspectives opening out on to the work which has been realized. In other words, the intrinsic value of a small-scale model is that it compensates for the renunciation of sensible dimensions by the acquisition of intelligible dimensions. (*The Savage Mind,* London 1966, pp. 23-24)

I have quoted this passage at length because it seems to me to point to one of the most vital features of Finlay's recent works: the manipulation and ironic modulation of scale. (It also, of course, reinforces the point about the models being hand-made.) Finlay has said that he was first attracted to the image of the aircraft carrier because of its combination of strength and vulnerability; and it has become in his work, in Stephen Bann's phrase, "the ultimate metaphor of elemental conflict." The key tactic in Finlay's treatment of military "hardware" has consisted of reducing it in scale in order to set it within unexpected contexts. The carrier reduced to a garden ornament becomes a bird-table, and the birds become planes (just as, in the print "Lullaby," the planes become birds.) The tortoise shell painted with the inscription "Panzer Leader" recalls a helmet accurately by its shape—but its speed, as opposed to that of a crack tank division, produces an ironic incongruity. As the images shuttle back and forth from one scale to another, they become interchangeable—but the reader/viewer never loses the awareness that at one end of the scale they are real, powerful, and deadly.

Nine of the twenty-six models in *The Boy's Alphabet Book* are military in origin. Set within the context of a book for boys, they evoke—in a manner as sophisticated as that of a *naif* painter—images of simple heroism, from an age when warfare could still be seen as simple and heroic. But beyond that "naive" level, the effect of the models is to distance, but not to eliminate, the reality of their destructive potential. The child's world is not one of idyllic innocence. *Et in Arcadia ego:* in the famous painting by Poussin, death is discovered at the centre of paradise. In Finlay's series of brilliant and unsettling reworkings of the pictorial theme, the tomb in the garden has become (the model of) a tank.

Finally, it should be noted that the models come to us through yet another layer of re-presentation and reduction: they come to us through Dave Paterson's photographs, which employ further tricks of scale, such as the silver-paper sea already mentioned, or the puffs of cigarette-smoke which simulate clouds behind the VI Flying Bombs.

When we attempt to put together all these various contexts, what we discover is an interplay of levels or codes of signification which is altogether more complex than the initial simplicity of the text would lead us to suppose. The "original" objects (i.e. the "real" boats, planes, guns, or even water-lilies) are filtered through the code of language (in the simple definitions), the code of literary convention (alphabet poems, primers, boys' books as opposed to girls' books), the code of literary allusion (echoes and reminiscences of other Finlay poems), the code of small-scale models (with all that that implies about perception and the effects of modulation of scale), and the code of photography (another reduction in scale, another "falsification" of the supposedly "real.") For the reader, the simplicity of the immediate textual level soon disappears in a dazzling interplay between all these other levels. On the left-hand page, a clear, direct, lucid verbal statement; on the right-hand page, a photograph of a model of an icon.

If a child's alphabet book serves as an introduction to the wonders and complexities of language, then Finlay's poem is a no less wonderful and complex introduction to a semiotic world in which the poetry lies in the activity which surrounds the text rather than in the text itself, a world in which the actual physical form of the book/pamphlet/carving/photograph acts as the major element of poetic form and poetic signification.

Note: Parts of this article appeared previously in a pamphlet published by the Graeme Murray Gallery, Edinburgh, as a catalogue to an exhibition of Finlay's work. They are re-published here by kind permission of Graeme Murray.

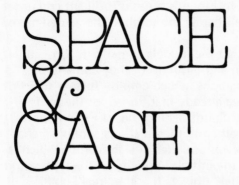

SPACE & CASE

by   Bolon Dzacab/Fred Truck

1

I did not write this essay, I collected it.
from the works of Marcel Duchamp
& the mathematician Rene Thom.

I display the words of Rene Thom
from STRUCTURAL STABILITY AND MORPHOGENESIS
which explain
the semantic origins of Marcel Duchamp's use
of 2-dimensional drawing & perspective
in THE BRIDE STRIPPED BARE BY HER BACHELORS, EVEN.

a new way might be here!

SHOW!

2

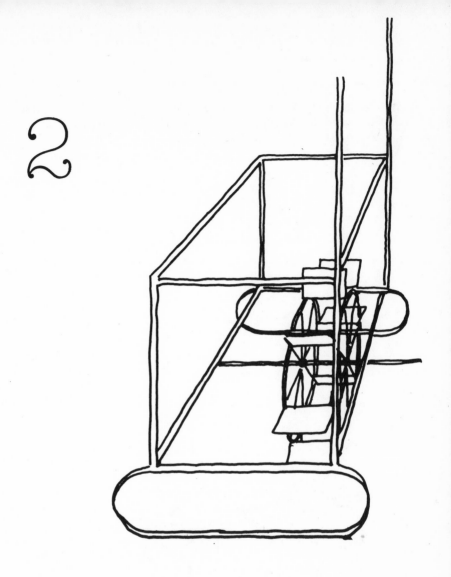

I n
the state of wakefulness, of continuous virtual predation, man can reach out
point sufficiently close to his body; and these voluntary movements give r
proprioceptive sensations which permit a rigorous metrical control o
displacement of limbs far more precise than the control of induced movements
we can assert that, very early in human development, there are local c
associated with the organism that describe all the metrical structure of Eucl
space.

Although the acquisition of a global appreciation of metrical space appears ea man, the same is not true of its representation by pictures.

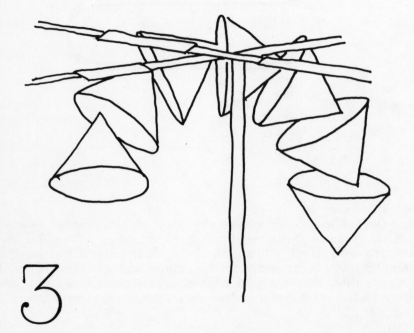

3

4

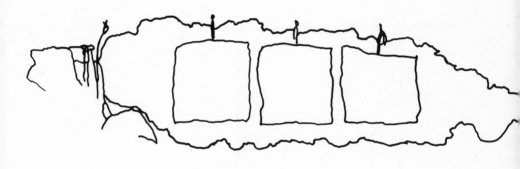

Dan

ve must concede that the universe we see is a ceaseless creation, evolution,
ction of forms and that the purpose of science is to forsee this change of form
possible, explain it.

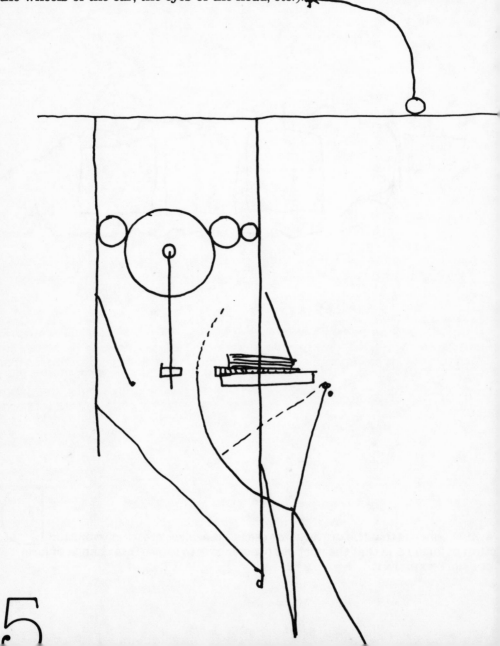

global chart of the object, the subobjects may be correctly located but drawn
own privileged perspective, thus explaining the phenomenon of flattening
Luquet has described in many designs by children. In such cases there is a
flict between the global perspective and the requirement of semantic dominance
n object over its subobjects. The relationships of surrounding, touching, and so
which are considered by Piaget as "topological," are in fact semantic relationships
dominance between concepts, relationships expressed precisely by the genitive
e (the wheels of the car, the eyes of the head, etc.).

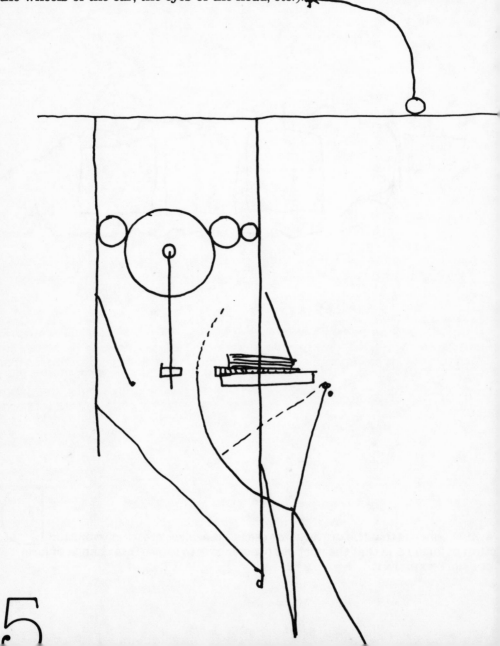

6

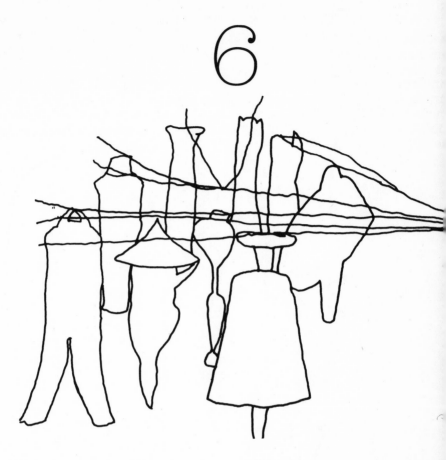

From where, then, does our feeling of beauty come? From the idea that the work of a is not arbitrary, and from the fact that, although upredictable, it appears to us have been directed by some organizing centre of large codimension, far from t normal structures of ordinary thought, but still in resonance with the ma emotional or genetic structures underlying our conscious thought. In this way t work of art acts like the germ of a virtual catastrophe in the mind of the behold

HOW IT WORKS IN ABC FORM

Bern Porter

> "I'm sorry I can read,"
> said Oscar Wilde on first
> seeing New York's night-
> lighted neon signs.

A. The eyes are for grasping,getting a hold on or fastening upon; certainly penetrating,even comprehending,knowing,understanding; above all feeling, *not* seeing.

B. To feel visually *is* the thing.

C. The inner spirit of things seen comes to the surface for the benefit of the beholder.

D. Let him who sees beware.

E. It is not the form in space,but the space around the form that defines,distills,lets go of the meaning.

F. Black is both elegant and subtle.

G. Let form effuse,bubble up,overflow,effloresce,sparkle,sing,shine brightly,reproduce itself many fold.

H. To feel a thing is to know it. (see also B.)

I. Soul sees and knows more than either eyes or mind.

J. Self interpretation is essential.

K. Content is more than significant:it is an integral part of the one seeing.

L. Good intent always radiates outward and for just reasons. (see also C.)

M. Potentialities for constructive use outweigh pernicious elements.

N. Pre-willed,purposeful statement is self perpetuating.

(juggle the order and re-read)

RAYMOND FEDERMAN'S VISUAL FICTION

Jerome Klinkowitz

If ever there were a writer who needed a visual form for his fiction to succeed, it would have to be Raymond Federman. Not that he lacks a story. Boy, does he have a story, and for many years he probably bored the ears off people with it. Born in France, a Jew, old enough to watch his family sent off to their deaths in a concentration camp while he, the young kid, was slipped out of the cattle car and cast loose to fate. Like his hero Beckett, he spent the war years working on an agricultural commune. Afterwards he spent two years of a young manhood scrambling and scuffling in Paris, finally contacting an uncle in the U.S. who helped him emigrate. At age eighteen he discovered America: scrambling and scuffling in New York and then Detroit, learning jazz with Detroit sidemen and once sitting in with Parker (swapping his tenor for Charlie's alto), joining the Army after the Navy rejected him as a Frogman (why not?), and so on.

It can be a good story, but not when you tell it. It needs something else. With his flamboyancy and vivid personal manner, Federman can sometimes enrich the telling sufficiently; but for many years the printed page was not adequate to what was really going on in Federman's narrative. It makes a damn boring novel in the conventional sense, as Federman found out. As a French major at Columbia in the Fifties (a tough one, huh, Raymond?), he wrote the one novel anyone can write but which no one else wants to read, a flat-out statement of his life story, called *And I Followed My Shadow*. It reads like *The Painted Bird* told by a garrulous veteran not too good with words. It gives all the details, all the persons and places, the whole damn story. And nobody cares. What's *your* story?

Thirty years after the events, and twenty years after he first tried to fictionalize them, Federman found the right approach: visual fiction. Once rolling, he won't stop, having told the same story four times over: *Double or Nothing* (Chicago: Swallow Press, 1971), *Amer Eldorado* (Paris: Editions Stock, 1974), *Take It Or Leave It* (New York: Fiction Collective, 1976), and *The Voice in the Closet* (Madison, WI: Coda Press, 1978). And each book is a visual and narrative joy—a story which can be told and retold as many times as Federman can practice his inventiveness. Visual forms are the key.

Double or Nothing is a photographed typescript, but what a typescript. Each page has its own form, and is done somewhat like a secretary's typewriter game, with words in the forms of Christmas trees, diagrams, and so forth. Part of Federman's inventiveness is finding appropriate forms, including maps and mazes, for the reader just when the story calls for them. But it's more than a trick. The reader is

forced to concentrate on the actual writing, or—better yet—typing;
it's impossible to fall through the words into the suspension of disbe-
lief in the story itself, which we know can't really sustain interest.
Moreover, we're vividly aware of the author composing his novel,
composing himself, as John Barth would pun. In fact, *Double or
Nothing* is not about the French adventure at all. It's about Raymond Federman sitting down to try writing the story. Thank God he
never succeeds.

Amer Eldorado (in French) and *Take It Or Leave It* (in Federman's
incomparable Americanese) uses visual means to tell another aborted
story, about the young GI's attempt to travel cross-country and discover America. He never makes it, and that's the best part of the
story. A third party is telling it, and the book responds with visual
equivalents: words breaking free of sentence lines to rank themselves
down the page (as the teller searches for the right term), exploding
like fireworks, cascading like Niagara Falls. Again, the purpose is not
just to please the eye, but to get the action on the page—something
more timid writers feel language (with its system of references) won't
let them do. Federman takes the referential and structural qualities
of language and uses them to show the artifice. Some day he might
write a novel with all the sentences diagrammed.

The Voice in the Closet is Federman's most interesting visual experiment. It has a square format, with its title (no author's name) in
black on a stark white cover. The text, in English, is set on the page,
in a frame of its own making, forming a perfect square. No hyphena-
tions (an old Federman discipline to force out bizarre synonyms fitting a 60-character line). On each double page, square graphics complement the square text. After twenty pages of this, the English text
ends, and you flip the book over and begin the French text, which is
probably Federman's most nerve-wracking achievement: same line
discipline, same "story," or so we think, again with all the words fitting a 60-character line! The joke is: either Federman has changed
the story, or he's found the deep structure of the Universe. Who
knows? The back cover, of course, has the title in French. Between
the two texts, Maurice Roche decomposes what Federman has written.

The typographical design is perfectly paginal, with a vengeance.
The page is the space of the rectangle of words. No caps, no punc-
tuations, nothing other than letters forming a geographical figure. The
speaking voice is that of fiction addressing Federman, the reverse of
his earlier books, accusing him of having screwed up the story. The
real story. The real story, of course, is the concentration camp, the
train, his dead family. Not telling that story has become, after four
books, Federman's new story.

PRINCIPLES OF CONCRETE STRUCTURALISM

John Jacob

Visual artists—or poets—or fiction writers—have concerned themselves with patterns of letters and words on paper as one obvious and
fairly acceptable means of expression. It probably does not indicate
anything new or radical in their artistic points of view that they
choose to undermine the basic structure of symbolic language as we
have come to know it, but the experimentation in these areas has
shown how inventive artists can be, and how often similar ideas really
differ radically from each other. Several structuralist critics and
thinkers have declared, in a parallelism close to the thought of pheno-
menological inquiry, that the reality of any structure resides in the
"speaker" himself. Translated to words deposited on a page, or letters incribed thereon, this statement suggests that the viewer becomes
the reader, and the reality is the information and point of view that
such a viewer brings to a work. If this is true, then, virtually infinite
variations can occur within any given structure—indeed, infinite
STRUCTURES may occur within any given locus of responses to
such a written work. But there is a great deal of contradictory evidence that an unusually small number of structures indeed are found
in so-called "concrete" literature. Certainly they cannot all be deline-
ated here, but several demand and are worthy of classification in order to supply more fully a terminology to other similar works. These
could be compared to taxonomic structures.

In many ways the most conventional "structure" applied to literature that relies on space and the dimensions of the page may be exem-
plified in such a work as Raymond Federman's *Double or Nothing.*
There is a strong narrative in the book, and that narrative seems capable of a full life oblivious to its form, had Federman chosen simply
to TELL A STORY. But the story he tells and the ways that he tells
that story differ even from each other, offering the reader an option
unavailable to him had Federman chosen a fictional narrative that did
not rely on his own peculiar typography. As it stands, the fact that
Swallow Press shot Federman's manuscript from his typescript alters
the way that the book makes its effect. Federman is never freed from
the burden of his own machine, from the idiosyncracies of light and
dark letters, from his obsessions or compunctions in composing on
the page itself. That he has prepared a meticulous manuscript seems
beside the point. He has taken a narrative and altered little more than
its presentation. The book is still narrative. Our demands on fictional
narrative still apply to the book. They are simply enriched or brought
down to earth or altered in some other less definable way by his technique.

In another context, Jacques Lacan has offered some interesting asides that might apply to Federman's book. The explicit narrative regarding the construction of a book within a book is extremely old, but Federman chooses it anyway. He compounds this desire to remind his reader of traditional literature by constantly referring to the work of writing at hand, almost never allowing the reader to immerse himself completely in the tale of the French boy who survives World War II, goes to Detroit, becomes a jazz musician, and then holes himself up in a room to write a book; or is that the story that some other persona has yet to invent? No matter. That is another inquiry entirely. What matters here is the type of communicatory device that Federman chooses, even when he decides the reader should read from right to left and bottom to top. As Lacan has it, "...a cryptogram takes on its full dimension only when it is in a lost language."

To mainstream readers of poetry and fiction, the works of Ian Hamilton Finlay constitute endeavor in a lost language, or at best a new invented language. But Federman's is never lost. It always is at hand, always stands the test of the familiar.

Any conventional ordering of thought can stand that test, or so it seems. These days, what may be needed are definitions of the conventional, the traditional, the usual. These definitions are almost always highly subjective, and may be completely useless. So if what is needed actually becomes what in reality is useless, then the field is open for new structures to assume the roles of their more known counterparts. What we may move toward is the radical and the unusual becoming the best-known or most available medium for expression. Richard Kostelanetz's fine poem ECHO, for instance, makes perfect sense when shown to six or seven-year-olds. It makes less and less conventional "sense" when shown to older viewers, and adult viewers usually regard it with a mixture of excitement and amusement: the point is that the adults do not know what it is, really, and they certainly do not know what to do with it. The uninitiated, the young, know completely what it is. And they also know that there is nothing to be done with it. It is there, and its presence is its use.

It is quite a step to suggest, therefore, that lost or cryptic language or structures will become the understood norm in written communication. But since education limits our understandings by what it imposes on us, and since socialization as a function of the educational process and vice versa remain so important in our world, testing this suggestion may be impossible. It is so now, and may always be.

We may at least move toward an understanding of a text such as Karl Young's *To Dream Kalapuya* (Truck Press), a book composed using "chance and spontaneous process." The book consists of clipped phrases and words holding their own on tiny pages. There is no field in which the letters interact with other orders of discourse.

In this sense, Young's book is much more conventional than Federman's. But it really is moving out on an axis of structure in which randomness is a determining factor in the interpretation of words and their meanings. Since many linguists would agree with the phenomenologists that connotation is at least as important to interpretation as denotation, chance occurrence and configurations determine both the real and the prodigiously individual meanings of the text that Young has apparently furnished at least partially by accident. His texts are drawn from a single source, and in that sense are highly and conventionally ordered; but his sense of narrative seems to coincide with none of that text, if his sense of narrative carries much of the burden of meaning in the text itself at all. Rather, the bouncing of letters off of letters begins here, and while most phrasings and even sentences make semantic English sense, the principle behind their amalgamation becomes much more of an experiment than that with which Federman concerned himself. We are slowly drifting, but very purposefully, on an axis toward a structuralism of texts.

At this point, neither Young nor Federman has offered the reader a lack of meaning as a principle, not in Lacan's sense anyway. Meaning being offered as a negative enterprise is important to our sense of structuralism, because it indicates a shift toward one of two undefined poles along this continuum of structures. A book which presses toward this end of the continuum is Ian Tarnman's *First Principles* (Future Press), in which the letter and the sign become synonymous, and either can become known as symbol. Symbology in Tarnman is unpredictable because it depends on Lacan's and Merleau-Ponty's sense of signified and signifier—so we almost cannot talk about it. A work such as "Red Shift" seems to offer Tarnman an infinite number of options apropos positioning of letters and their variations, their shadows. Such is hardly the case, however. The unusually high number of interpretations the text elicits depends entirely on Tarnman's ability to remove most narrative from his text, from his work. And as he embarks upon this disintegration of narrative, he propounds structure. It seems ironic that the artists who are called rebels in our artistic, if not our social, worlds frequently mean to return us to those days when definable commodities at least existed, even if they could not be pegged and pinpointed. Tarnman invests his texts with divestitures. As Lacan puts it, "using the reverberating character of meaning to invest it with the desire aimed at the very lack it supports" can easily be viewed as one of the foci of Tarnman's conceptual poetry.

The final word on structuralism of this sort cannot be narrative, again, because of that lack of definition. The final word *can,* perhaps, be "availability" in the sense of availability to traditional expectations. After all, it is our locus of expectations that is upset by these works, not our implicit sense of narrative, since it is at best moot whether we have any such implicit sense. And since expectations are built and are constantly changing, this axis constructed by viewing three unusual works of literature must constantly shift to accommodate other points of view and attitudes—and other texts. Hopefully, texts will be able to be fit into/onto this continuum, but it is more reasonable that other texts will fall off the axis and plummet into space until grabbed by the helpful hand of a structuralist or a visual composer himself.

If we begin with underminings, we end with underpinnings. These artists do not fool with us so much as they fool with themselves; that is the principal beauty of such art, and the principal source of its misunderstanding.

Raymond Federman

```
WHY --------------------- WHY
          MAURICE ROCHE
WHY --------------------- WHY
```

What to say to what is skimpy / shabby / contemptuous (involuntarily?)?

Say what you think? (first error!) ---- say it obscenely (second error!):

Bugger off
Leave us rest in peace!

Make us tremble before/behind because of the context

Social in its compact form: the cassock   hier
                                               ket
Face to the inquisitor to be put through the wringer
                                 to the test

ANSWER!

An ASS ... HEY!

D-DAY   HEE! Haw! Hee!   HAW! Hellabaloo!
Amalgamate yourselves
take, like a good democrat, all positions simultaneously!
Amalgamate yourselves
well in your poses and eternal reposes --   PAUSE

(Funeral Cantata)

MAURICE ROCHE what guts: *Compact / Circus / Codex*
                          Opera Bouffe
                          Memoire   unreadable books
                                               (*in any language*)
                                               they say!

But those who say that have never learned how to read!

(*I listen only for the pleasure of repeating* -- DI-de-ROT)   Unreadability
                                          is the excuse of the lazy!

Those who ask that books communicate
something merely want to be reassured
in what they already know ------------ (*there is no communication because
                        there are no vehicles of communication* -- Be-QUETTE)!

(-- *can't you see he repeats any dumb thing he hears without understanding it.
All he needs is to hear it once.*
(-- *he has to hear it to be able to repeat it* (replied MAURICE). *have you ever
been able to say a dumb thing which you would have found yourself?* -- QUEUE-
                                                              NEAU)!

Must I explain?   Let us explain!

V(0)I(C)E(S) within V()I(C)E(S)

Process of displacement: to take written texts -- poems/fictions --
already fixed set printed in one place. AUTHOR-ized by a name (in
this case MAURICE ROCHE) Finished (?) Temporarily finished (non,
even printed, words refuse totalization). To relocate these into
other spaces: ORAL/ VISUAL.

                              (*The possibility if/or of displacement*)
                              (*is found in the very nature of langua*)
                              (*ge in the fact that language is seman*)
                              (*tic that is in the vibration or movem*)
                              (*ent that surrounds the words and whic*)
                              (*h no dictionary (French or English or*)
                              (*even Javanese) will ever succeed in r*)
                              (*endering the possibility of displacem*)
                              (*is found in the play of meaning or/if*)

Process of cancellation: to annul written texts -- poems/fictions --
pregnant with signification. To remove by superimposition by double
exposure (doubletalk: bilingual and multilingual) the established
meaning of words: the something-to-be-said that always pretends
to be there even before texts are written. Blur meaning xxxxxx

by mixxxxxing voices. The signal of a single voice multiplied by itself
(or vice versa): in this case MAURICE ROCHE's voice speaking within itself.

> more and more we have come to recognize
> that art cancels itself the tinguely ma
> machine works to destroy itself the bla
> nk page and the white canvas pretend to
> deny their existence   more and more
> modern music abolishes itself into sile
> nce or discordance fiction poetry write
> themselves into non-sense or lessnessne

radical irony
implicit in the statement of the old Cretan
                            who affirms that all
                Cretans
are liars   thus cancelling
                          with one or two
both the $t_{r_{u_{t_h}}}$ & the $l^{i^e}{}_l$ $\ell\,\ell$ of this
perfect rhetorical statement!

Process of pulverization: to decompose written texts -- poems/fictions --
already organized into a form a structure a syntax (ah yes a syntax!) oops!
Stylized by a name: in this case MAURICE ROCHE. To destructure words in
their syntactical unity by dissemination. Oral/visual dslioctaition: $d^i s_l$
$a^{co}{}_{t_i{}^o{}_n}$

echoooooes that designify language --- here
                        the designword
                        and the designsyntax   (independent
                                                     of one ano-
                    are set against   ther)
                            one
                        another!

(syntax, traditionally, is the unity, the continuity of words, the law which)
(dominates them, it reduces their multiplicity, controls their violence, and)
(it fixes them into a place, a space, prescribes an order to them, it preven)
(ts them from wandering, even if it is hidden, it reigns always on the horiz)
(on of words which buckle under its mute exigency so says michel FOU-cault!!)

Process of repetetititetion: to rererepeat written texts -- poems/fictions --
AUTHOR ized / by overlapping (orally but also visually) with slight VARIA ^{DEVIA} tions
AUTEUR $d^i{}_s{}_t{}_o{}^r{}_t{}_i{}_o{}^n{}_s$ (i-r-o-n-i-e-s?) in an attempt to prevent unity of
PRESENCE!

> The Author (in this case MAURICE ROCHE) is (perhaps) that
> which gives the *sic* disquieting language of poetry/fiction
> its unities its knot of coherence its insertion into the real.

we listen only for the pleasure of repeating
and yet we write under the illusion that we
are not repeating what has already been said

> to tell or retell, to make or
> remake works on the principle
> of duplication and repetition

memory does not separate itself from imagination or if it does it is only a
slight displacement of facts/lies/facts/lies!

Process of revision: to rewrite (collectively preferably) texts seemingly
static in their written form. Speaking/reading words of others -- in this
case MAURICE ROCHE's -- is to rewrite. To listen to words/look at words
already frozen on the page is to RE-write
                    DE-write.   Therefore the writer is no
longer to be considered a prophet a philosopher or even a sociologist who
predicts teaches reveals absolute truths nor is he to be looked upon (oh
so admiringly/romantically) as the omnipotent/scient/present/omni creat
or but must now stand on equal footing with the reader/listener in an
effort to make sense out of the language common to both of them (here and now)!

to write, in this sense, orally/visually, is always to rewrite, and to rewrite does not mean to revert to a previous form (or syntax) of writing, no more than to an an teriority of speech, or of presence, or o f meaning. to rewrite: undoubling which a lways precedes unity, or suspends it whil e pla(y)giarizing it. to rewrite is perfo rmed apart from all productive initiative and does not pretend to produce anything!

not even the past, or the future, or the pr esent of writing. to rewrite while repeati iiiiiiing what does n ot, will not, in fact did not take place, i nscribes itself in an immense non-unified s ystem of relations wh ich

intersect without having any point of intersection affir
m the coincidence, thus inscribing itself under the exig
ency of return by which we are pulled away from the modes of temporality w
hich are always measured by a unity of presence (here and everywhere now!!

Process of self-pla(y)giarization: to re-play texts by inserting them into
other texts. InTerTexTuaLizaTion: in this case MAURICE ROCHE's imagination
plagiarizing itself. to pla(y)giarize one's li^f_fe -- voices within vices!

Oh free me now of the never endingutterance!

The deaf writes: *Today I have sharpen my voice, lubricated the organ of*
                  phonation of the yellow of a raw egg!   Answer below
                                                               in CAPITAL
                                                               letters . . .

Louder : AH AH AH!


```
        MAURICEMAURICE       MAURICEMAURICE
        MAURICE  MAURICE     MAURICE  MAURICE
        MAURICE  MAURICE     MAURICE  MAURICE
        MAURICE  MAURICE MAURICE      MAURICE
        MAURICE  MAURICEMAURICE       MAURICE
        MAURICE                       MAURICE
        MAURICE                       MAURICE
        MAURICE          ROCHE        MAURICE
                         ROCHEROCHE
                         ROCHEROCHEROCHE
                         ROCHEROCHE
                         ROCHE
```

CONCRETE TREATMENT OF SPACE

Roland Grass

Aural art involves temporal organization; visual art involves spatial organization. In a period when music is often concerned with creating an illusion of space in unexpected silences (in the manner of Webern, for example) and when painting may be concerned with temporal sequence (as in Mondrian's "Boogie-Woogie" series, for example), it is easy to lose sight of the fundamental nature of these arts. But there is some evidence that aural space exists only in the realm of analogy. Victor Zuckerkandl has pointed out that pitch is not universally referred to as "high" or "low." In Greek, for example, the respective words are *sharp* and *heavy*. Zuckerkandl reminds us that English, too, has *sharp* and *flat* and that these words have no clear spatial connotations.[1] I myself have heard a child refer to the high register of a piano as "bright" and the low register as "dark." Although I cannot cite an example, I would not be surprised to hear one speak of high pitch as "near" and low pitch as "far." In a similar way it is doubtful that Andy Warhol's multiple images (the cinema notwithstanding) would be viewed in the same sequence in a culture that reads from right to left as in one that reads from left to right (not to mention a culture that reads as the ox plows a field or one that reads not at all).

So a poetry, like concrete poetry, that, in our print culture, concentrates on the visual image on the printed page is likely to be concerned substantially with space. Even a poet like Eugen Gomringer, when he wishes to concretize an aural phenomenon like silence, relies on a spatial analogy. If silence is an absence of sound, this fact may be suggested graphically by surrounding an open space with the word (in this case in Spanish) that means "silence" (see fig. 1). Conversely, in oral poetry the illusion of space may be created by periods of silence.

I should like to deal here with the concretization of space in three concrete poems by different authors. These poems communicate primarily through the visual image—that is, the image that the poem itself makes on the page. One of them is constructed of the three syllables of the Portuguese word for *space,* "espaço," arranged in a decorative pattern (fig. 2). Another is constructed of the Italian word for *space,* "spazio." In this case the illusion of a third dimension is created through the use of different type sizes (fig. 3). The third poem consists only of a small black square and relies on its title in Serbo-Croatian, "Pesma o Prostoru," to indicate that it is a "Poem about Space" (fig. 4).

For purposes of comparison I have included a pencil drawing by
Richard Law, entitled,"Space Structure" (fig. 5). I include this drawing for two related reasons. A comparison will show, I believe, that
the concrete poems that I am dealing with here (my observations do
not apply to *all* works called concrete poems) function effectively as
graphic art rather than through linguistic processes. Language is used
only to clarify the theme of the piece as a title may be used to speci-
fy the theme of a graphic work. (An admirable feature of two of
these poems is that they use the word that identifies their theme to
construct the image. The implications of this method are, I believe,
rich and complex; but, as far as the eye is concerned, nonalphabetic
shapes could be used to produce the same effect.) The title of
Richard Law's drawing is exemplary: It indicates that the drawing is
about *space* and it implies that space has a *structure.* My second
reason for including the drawing here is that I think that more than
coincidence is involved in the fact that two of the concrete poems included here represent space in essentially the same way that the drawing does.

If one assumes, as I do, that all three of these poets and the artist
were working independently of each other, one can draw some interesting (and, I believe, meaningful) inferences from the various works.
The square shape I take to be important. On one level it is necessary
to construct a frame in order to confine (or define) space, in the same
way that Eugen Gomringer found it necessary to frame an open area
in order to create an analogue of silence. But two of these works in-
sist on the essential squareness of the image by representing a square
within the square of the frame—Richard Law's drawing (fig. 5) and
Arrigo Lora Totino's concrete poem (fig. 3).

The fact that all three poets and the artist developed essentially
square forms suggests the possibility that all four (consciously or not)
relied on the square shape to communicate by means of conventional
symbolism. In conventional symbolism space is associated with the
four cardinal points of the compass, which themselves imply the
square.[2] But in addition, as J.E. Cirlot observes, the square may be
identified with various conventional meanings of the number four and
has fairly specific psychological implications: "The square, as the expression of the quaternary, is a symbol of the combination and regulation of four different elements. Hence, it corresponds to the symbolism of the number four and to all four-part divisions of any process
whatsoever. Psychologically, its form gives the impression of firm-
ness and stability, and this explains its frequent use in symbols of organization and construction" (p. 292).

These rather wholesome implications of the square, in terms of
conventional symbolism, are given some support by another aspect of
two of the poems and the drawing. In Pedro Xisto's poem (fig. 2) the

syllables of the word *espaço* function in at least three ways (in addition to establishing the theme of the poem): they define the essentially square shape of the frame, they establish a regular pattern within the frame, and they suggest particles that fill the frame. Essentially the same functions are performed by the letters of the word *spazio* in Arrigo Lora Totino's poem (fig. 3) and by the pencil marks in Richard Law's drawing (fig. 5). In the last two works, the illusion of a third dimension contributes further to the overall impression of stability and order. It may not be inappropriate to point out that inferences consistent with the findings of modern particle physics may be drawn from the concrete poems of Pedro Xisto and Arrigo Lora Totino.

In contrast, certain aspects of Miroljub Todorović's little poem (fig. 4) make one wonder if it is to be taken seriously. It has the square shape of the other two poems and the drawing, with the attendant potentiality for conventional symbolism. But the image is too small (5/32" x 5/32") for the size of its original page (5½" x 7 13/16"), and the solid black square suggests an attitude of nihilism or frivolity (or both). I must recognize, of course, that these suggestions do not necessarily exhaust the possible meanings of Todorović's little square, nor do I wish to imply that an expression of nihilism may not be appropriate to him.

At one time or another I have entertained the notion that a fundamentally visual poetry like concrete poetry may have overtones of nihilism or anarchy. The Lettrists, who have been treated along with the Concretists, in explaining why they believe it to be necessary to reduce poetry to its most fundamental element, the letter of the alphabet, stated in the first number of their review: "It is not a question of destroying words in order to create other words, but of concretizing silence, of writing nothing."[3] About as much can be said for Todorović's poem included here. On the other hand, Eugen Gomringer's poem (fig. 1), which is, indeed, a concretization of silence, somehow manages to avoid similar implications of nihilism. Gomringer's poem and the poems by Pedro Xisto and Arrigo Lora Totino may be taken to represent the serious purpose and effective communicability of concrete poetry.

Notes

[1] Victor Zuckerkandl, *Sound and Symbol: Music and the External World,* trans., Willard R. Trask (New York: Pantheon, 1956), p. 86.

[2] See J.E. Cirlot, *A Dictionary of Symbols* (New York: Philosophical Library, 1962), p. 287.

[3] See Guillermo de Torre, *Historia de las literaturas de vanguardia* (Madrid: Guadarrama, 1965), pp. 745-46. Cf. Isidore Isou, "The Creations of Lettrism," *The Times Literary Supplement,* 3 Sept. 1964, p. 796.

silencio   silencio   silencio
silencio   silencio   silencio
silencio   silencio
silencio   silencio   silencio
silencio   silencio   silencio

Figure 1. Eugen Gomringer (Switzerland, born in Bolivia). "Silencio"
[Silence] , ca. 1956 (?). Reproduced by Mary Ellen Solt, *Concrete Poetry: A World View* (Bloomington: Indiana Univ. Press, 1970), p. 91.

          es   *pa*   *ço*
      es   *pa*   *ço*   *es*
          pa   *ço*   *es*
      pa   *ço*   *es*   *pa*
          ço   *es*   *pa*
      ço   *es*   *pa*   *ço*
          es   *pa*   *ço*

Figure 2. Pedro Xisto (Brazil). "Espaço" [Space] . *Hai-Kais & Concretos [Haiku & Concrete Poems]* (ca. 1960). Reproduced by Guillermo de Torre, *Historia de las literaturas de vanguardia* (Madrid: Guadarrama, 1965), p. 757.

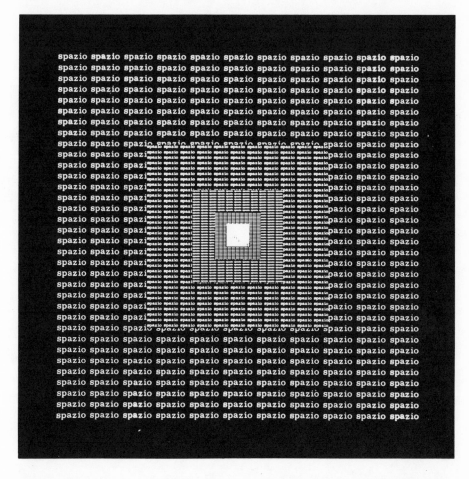

Figure 3. Arrigo Lora Totino (Italy). "Spazio" [Space], n.d. Reproduced by Mary Ellen Solt, *Concrete Poetry: A World View* (Bloomington: Indiana Univ. Press, 1970), p. 187.

PESMA O PROSTORU

Figure 4. Miroljub Todorović (Yugoslavia). "Pesma o Prostoru" [Poem about Space]. *Stepenište [Staircase]* (Belgrade: Signalističko Izdanje, n.d. [ca. 1971]), p. [78].

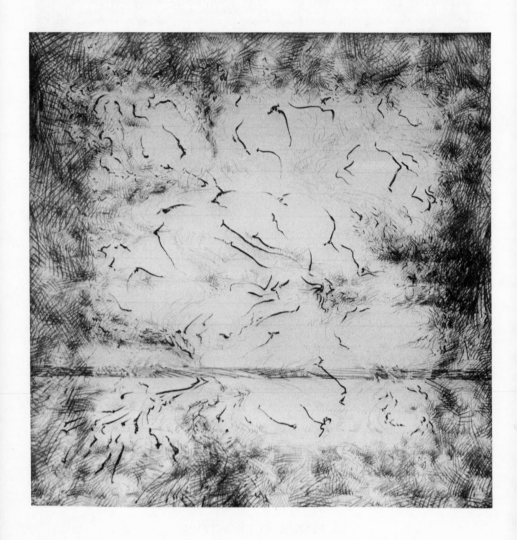

Figure 5. Richard Law (United States). "Space Structure." 1971,
pencil, 23 x 23".

VISUAL POETRY AS A MOLTING

Geoffrey Cook

1.

In my essay, "Visual Poetry" which appeared in *La Mamelle Art Contemporary* (Vol. 2, #4), I pointed out that visual poetry has appeared four times in Occidental art history as an extensive movement —during the Alexandrine period, the Carolingian renaissance, the Baroque, & our own day. I further pointed out that these were times of literary decadence & Mannerist propensities, & that VisPo was/is a sign of the decadence & the decadence resolving itself (piercing the cycle) into "something else." A further insight inclines me to write that each of the past three incarnations appeared at the death of one cultural epoch & the beginning of another. Visual poetry is a cry by the poet that the content of the past is cancerous & a new skin must be sewn to contain the dreams of the future—a visual statement that nothing more meaningful can be said till we can restructure the basic vision that is an historical culture.

2.

If anything the visual poetry collected in a forthcoming anthology denies that the new culture will be the repository for any one national or ethnic tradition. This new cultural vision is international. Personally, I feel more in common with the work being done in Brazil and Eastern Europe than with most of my neighbors involved in the parochial concerns of the San Francisco art & literary "worlds" where I happen to reside. And, I'm sure that my colleagues in Recife and Berlin—& all those other places on our planet where they reside & work —find that 90% of their fellow local artists are reactionary, dull, & provincial. Because of technology a truly international & progressive art movement(s) is(are) possible. Visual poets were one of the first groups to take advantage of this new state of affairs, for poets traditionally have been attached to the book & broadside—two of the cheapest & most accessible means of display & distribution. Mail art has furthered communication between artists & has even freed the individual from the editor/writer tyranny—which has traditionally been a damper to highly innovative work. Also, inexpensive printing has encouraged the artist's book (a book which is usually within the control of the artist at all points of production). In fact the visual poet has been the innovator in forms & experiments which the other artists are now emulating. The international VisPo movement is now building the structures for the future art world.

3.

Walter Benjamin in a favorite essay of mine, "The Work of Art in the Age of Mechanical Reproduction," discusses the Dadaists of the Cabaret Voltaire days as coming upon aesthetic problems before the technological means to resolve them appeared. What was anti-art to the general public of 1916 became in the cinema of 1924, the comic art of Chaplin & Buster Keaton. Further, two of the majors trends of Modernism—Dadaism & Futurism—were almost "purged" from the living traditions of Western art (at least in America) due to historical/ political circumstances. Most of the Dadaists & Futurists became either Fascists or Communists or were liquidated in the European civil conflict which we call the Second World War. The Surrealists escaped from Paris to New York; Max Ernst married Peggy Guggenheim; & the Expressionists were emulated in America (& most especially New York) for being politically right. America was the big winner in World War II (for it was the only major industrialized country not totally exhausted), &, therefore, inherited the cultural hegemony of the West by default. The McCarthy purges further discouraged studies & contacts with aesthetic ideas that smacked of the surviving leftist ideologies (such as Mayakovsky & the Russians). *Ergo,* Expressionism & Surrealism mixed with indigenous North American aesthetic thinking was to dominate the Western world for two decades. In the '60's the Fluxus group was the first crack in this cultural egg. This movement began to reinvestigate those other trends of Modernism. Out of this initial revolt came concrete poetry in Europe & process poetry in Brazil. During this decade the crack in New York's cultural hegemony has become a rift. Art is & can be created vitally anywhere on the globe. There is no one center. Dadaism & Futurism have been reinvestigated in a context that is coming to terms with the technological innovations of the past six decades. Language is further being investigated structurally & sociologically. As Dick Higgins says, "The word is not dead, it is merely changing its skin."

A BOOK OF HOURS/A LOG BOOK/A WORKBOOK/A PSALTER/
A BOOK OF KATUNS/A BOOK OF ETIQUETTE/
A PALIMPSEST/A CUMULATIVE RECORD/A HYMNAL/
A DICTIONARY/A SKETCHBOOK/A MISSAL/A GUIDEBOOK/
A PATTERN BOOK/AN ALBUM/A CRIB/A DAY BOOK/
A THESAURUS/A CATALOGUE/A BOOK OF PROPHECIES/
A CODEX/A PRIMER/A DIARY/A TONALAMATL/
A SCRAPBOOK/AN INDEX/A CODE BOOK/A NOTEBOOK/
AN ILLUMINATED BOOK/A PILLOW BOOK/
A CIPHER/A TESTAMENT

Karl Young

Offset printing is sometimes referred to as a form of planographic printing—transferring an image from one planar surface to another. The objects printed on are thin sheets—not, say, solid cubes or cones —and a number of parts of the press and its accessories are also planar; they approximate two dimensional objects. One of the main abilities of thin sheets in offset printing is that, if made of paper, neoprene, or certain kinds of metal, they can be formed into cyclinders. Basically an offset press is a system of cylinders constructed in such a way as to handle sheets and sheetlike phenomena. A press, in abstract, consists of two sets of rollers, a set of cyclindrical drums, a system for bringing these together and passing paper through them. One set of rollers, the inking system, is a set of cylinders that picks up ink from a trough, grinds it and smoothes it out into a forward-moving sheet of ink that eventually comes in contact with a metal plate fastened so as to form a continuously repetitive surface over a cylindrical drum made of a heavier metal. Another set of rollers, the water system, is set up to bring a sheet of water-gum-acid solution into contact with the plate at roughly the same time as the sheet of ink. It is here that the alchemy of offset printing begins: ink and water repel each other in much the same way as water and oil repel each other. The surface of the plate has been photochemically altered in such a way that certain areas—the image areas—are receptive to ink and repellent to water and other areas—the non-image areas—are repellent to ink and receptive to water. The ink and water sheets brought into contact with the plate can be balanced to a degree of fineness that allows the natural antipathy between water and ink to hold the shape of an image so small it can be seen only with a magnifying glass—and hold it perfectly within its own bounds. Nearly every printed photograph you see was created by this balanced antipathy on a minute scale: if you look at a printed photograph through a magnifying glass, you'll see it is made up of thousands of tiny dots. If the picture doesn't look right

to you, if it's blurry, or indistinct, or muddy, there's a good chance
that these dots are inexact in one way or another—and one of the
things that can make these dots inexact is an imbalance of ink and
water in the printing process.

From the plate image, ink is transferred to the blanket, which is a
sheet of neoprene wrapped around another metal cylinder that by a
system of gears at its edges and the edges of the plate cylinder turns
against the plate cylinder. As the image is transferred it is reversed—
the image you'll see on the blanket will be a mirror image of that on
the plate. Paper is stacked at one end of the press and fed through a
system of air pressures and tapes up to the cylinders. It passes between the blanket cylinder and another cylinder, the impression cylinder, which is also turned against the blanket cylinder by a system of
gears. Here the ink is transferred, being reversed a second time in the
transfer. Remember what happens to double negatives: this second reversal makes it come out on the page as it originally was, with words
running from left to right. The printed paper is then deposited in
another stack at the other end of the press.

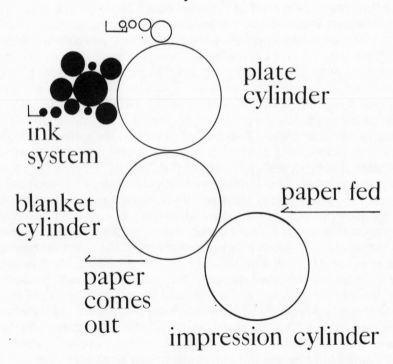

I.   Diagram of an offset press, side view.

One can imagine into what ecstasies knowledge of such a process would send the Renaissance philosophers John Dee or Giordano Bruno. Offset printing appeals to my more arcane and esoteric tendencies in the same way that other aspects of the process appeal to my need for manual work, my desire for making images, my hopes for craftsmanship, etc. Since early in my experience with offset printing, I've wanted to make works of print art that reflect the process itself. This is the first element, the basic drive behind the development of these big books with the long titles.

In the offset printing process, there are many operations that can only be performed by running sheets of ink and water over their rollers, engaging the gears in the transfer of inked image, and then feeding paper from one stack to the other. Most important here is establishing the balance of ink and water described above. At the beginning of a day's work, you adjust the ink-water ratio—partly from habit but also from the process of feeding paper through and looking at the sheets that come out the delivery end of the press. Sometimes this can be done relatively quickly, using only a few sheets of paper; at other times it takes longer and more paper gets used. The ink-water ratio must sometimes be readjusted as you go along: for instance, a new balance must be established if you have been printing something requiring a lot of ink. If the balance is lost, poor print quality results; most commonly this is manifested by scum, bits of ink that appear in non-image areas when ink is too heavy, or ghosting, fading around the edges of an image or the appearance of a gray nimbus around an image, when you're running too much water. When this happens the process must be repeated to restore proper balance.

Establishing register—getting the image exactly where you want it on the page—also requires printing: you print a sheet or two, make adjustments, print some more, examine what you've printed, etc. until the image is where you want it. For vertical registration (registration this way: ↑ or↓), you move the blanket cylinder in relation to the plate cylinder so the image from the plate is transferred to a different place on the blanket cylinder and hence a different position on the page. When you then print, some of the ink from the former impression remains for a few copies, while new ink is transferred to the new position: hence your printed sheets will have increasingly less ink in the old position until all the ink from the old position has been transferred off the blanket and the correct amount of ink is transferring from the new position. Horizontal registration (this way: ←or→) requires moving the feedboard and does not create multiple images as does vertical registration: the paper moves, so the image appears in a different place on it, but the blanket does not move.

Sometimes you have to adjust the feeding mechanism and this too requires feeding paper through the press.

The most economical way of making these adjustments is to use scrap paper—paper that has been incorrectly printed in the past—for these operations. As you go along, such sheets pile up—you can set them aside and merely put some of them at the top of the feeding stack when an adjustment has to be made. Such sheets can be reused many times.

After a day's printing, the press should be cleaned. One way of doing this is by the use of clean-up sheets—heavy, absorbent sheets of paper you wrap around the plate cylinder in place of the plate. When one of these is in place, you start the press, apply solvent to the rollers, and allow the ink to transfer onto the clean-up sheet. This is repeated several times until all the ink has been removed from the rollers. The first sheet takes up the most ink; the following sheets take up successively less—so the first sheet is dark and heavy with ink and the last is lightly inked—as though lightly stained. One result of this process is that used clean-up sheets accumulate in your workroom if you don't throw them away.

I don't know for sure when I first started thinking of using scrap sheets in books—but it seems to have been in the early seventies when I was working at a shop called Wisconsin Speed Press. Around 1972 I acquired my own press—a used A.T.F. Chief 17. As I worked in my own shop, reused scrap sheets and clean-up sheets accumulated. The first definite idea I can remember for their use was circa 1973, when I thought I'd cut clean-up sheets in half and send them in to ASSEM-BLING, I think for the fourth issue. But I hadn't yet accumulated enough of them to provide several for each copy, so I shelved the idea for the time being.

Time passed and sheets accumulated. I gave a few clean up sheets to friends as novelties and put a few of the multiply-printed scraps up on my own walls. As time went by I kept thinking of ways to make printed art that would emphasize the offset process and come direct-ly out of it. Most of these were poorly conceived, or were unproduce-able using my own equipment. One of the things I wanted to do was to create books that would contain surprises for me, things I couldn't have predicted before the books were finished. My main line of think-ing involved use of computers, multiple participants, etc.

In March of 1973 Jackson Mac Low came to Milwaukee for a per-formance-reading-visit. I suggested to him that perhaps my press could be used as a tool in systematic-chance generation of poems. He said he thought it was an interesting idea but didn't come up with a program and we didn't do anything with the idea while he was in Mil-waukee. But thinking about using the press to generate poems through systematic-chance processes was the main factor in getting me to work on the big books. I realized that I had been producing systematic-chance generated works all along with my reuse of scrap. I'd even made use of some of these for specific purposes already: accidents that happened in the process of reusing scrap had suggested designs and methods for designing book covers and graphics. (On this, cf. cover and endpapers of Toby Olson's *Home,* the cover of my *Questions and Goddesses* and the whole text of my forthcoming books, *A Book of Openings* and *Second Book of Omens.*) Curiously enough, at this time I began consciously working with the process: when I needed to reuse some scrap I sometimes selected scrap sheets I thought would work interestingly with the image currently on the press, though I seldom spent much time planning this out—I usually just impulsively fed things into the press and didn't check the results till I had to go through the stack in collating or packaging. This moderated the chance element in the final work.

During the spring of 1975, I decided to do these books pretty much in the form in which they now appear. But I procrastinated through the rest of 1975 and the first months of 1976. The first books in both series were completed in June, 1976.
   A description of the first two series of books follows:

SERIES ONE: BOOK OF BOOKS — for Jackson Mac Low, 10¾" x 8 3/8" x 2 5/8", approx. 600pp.
Books in this series are made up of reused scrap with multiple images printed on the sheets. These books contain material I'd break down into 5 categories. Sometimes the individual pages fit more than one category. The categories are:
1. Interesting images: more of each book is of this sort than any other. Gut response to books in this series is almost wholly on this level.
2. Subtractive texts: texts produced when one text is superimposed over another so that all but discrete areas of either text are illegible: the fragmented text occurs where there's no overlap and a few words are revealed. Cf. my fragment pieces and Tom Phillips' *A Humument.*
3. Additive texts: texts produced when one text is superimposed over another and both texts remain legible. This usually occurs when the lines of one of the texts fall between or around the lines of the other or when the lines are in different colors. Cf. Jackson Mac Low's AS-SYMETRIES.
4. Collages: when several texts or images more or less maintain their integrity and form new works by being placed next to each other.
5. Stains: these are the result of a different process and occur simultaneously with other categories. I put sheets down in various places to catch drips; the drips and resultant spreading stains interact with the images under them.

One of the things I like most about this series of books is their sequence of pages. Few sequences of pages were consciously planned
out, whether the individual pages were selected intentionally or by
chance processes. I love repetition and most of my work involves
one form of it or another. The numbers of image elements in the
books are limited: what I printed between the time I got my press
and the time I made the particular book. Most operations requiring
the running of scrap require the running of a number of sheets per
image—sometimes quite a few—and the mistakes that consign sheets
to the reusable scrap heap sometimes go on for a while before being
detected. Hence images recur—often in different positions and in different relations to other images—and these other images are usually
different images. This gives the books a polyphonal, almost fugue-
like quality. As I go through one of the books, I see that some images
remain almost tonal constants, others recur at regular intervals. A
few images intensify this by appearing only once. This constancy
and change, repetition through metamorphosis seems to me to be one
of the half-dozen basic forms of any art.

I mentioned above the desire to create books that would contain
surprises even for me. These books are full of such surprises—I still
find new things in the first book I made over two years ago.

SERIES TWO: MINING RAINBOWS — 10¾" x 8 3/8" x 2 5/8", ap-
rox. 300pp.
The pages of these books consist of used clean-up sheets. They are
books generally without words. Here and there a heavily inked word
or two may transfer back from the blanket onto the clean-up sheet or
a few words will transfer onto the clean-up sheet from the plate cylinder when I have used two-sided plates. But these cases are rare.

The clean-up sheets have their own special colors you won't see
quite the same anywhere else. I suppose this is partly because so
much ink gets on them and because they absorb the ink so deeply.
Anyway, the beauty of these colors is the first thing people experience when looking at these books. The major significance of these
books is simply to attract attention to and encourage concentration
on these colors.

In a sense these sheets represent to me an expression, a mapping, of
the subconscious of the press. Because ink can be applied over these
total areas, an enormous variety of images can be printed. In much
the same way as a Renaissance sculptor could claim that the form of a
sculpture was latent in the marble and that his job was simply to free
that latent form, I sometimes see printing as a freeing of images,
through the balance of water and ink from the total black or red or
whatever colored sheet of ink that is my raw material. In a sense,
then, everything I'll ever print is latent in these images. And in a similar sense, everything I've ever printed has returned to these sheets in

the clean-up process. These sheets then are a manifestation of what you might want to call the basic ground of being—at once empty and full—from which all forms come and to which they all return.

These books are made up of things that for me are everyday objects but are oddities to most of the people who see them. I print books and these sheets are an important part of that process; most people who see the books do not print and these objects are not in their quotidian vocabularies of objects. For me there is a strange sort of interpenetration of the strange and the familiar in these books—perhaps because they're so bulky or perhaps because they're unlike most of the books I produce and most of the books I use.

One interesting extra dimension to this series of books is that the clean-up sheets retain some of the smell of the ink and solvent that went into them. You've probably noticed the smell of a new book, which is essentially the same sort of smell—but in this case the smell is much stronger and more pungent.

The type for the covers of both series was set using 11 point type on a composer setting for 7 point type (lucky numbers). As a result, the characters are squeezed together, sometimes the strokes of one letter joining those of its neighbor, serifs blending into each other, etc. This gives them something of the character of the uncial hand used in medieval illuminated manuscripts. The books are very much like such manuscripts: they were made by a long slow process, each volume is unique (which is why I list each kind as a series—there are no duplicates, though each volume in a series is put together according to the principle of that series), the volumes combine text and illustration in a fused state hard to produce by any other means, etc. As the ordinary and the strange interpenetrate each other in these books, so do the newest characteristics of bookmaking wander in and out of the oldest.

A Book of Hours	A Day Book
A Log Book	A Thesaurus
A Workbook	A Catalogue
A Psalter	A Book of Prophecies
A Book of Katuns	A Codex
A Book of Etiquette	A Primer
A Palimpsest	A Diary
A Cumulative Record	A Tonalamatl
A Hymnal	A Scrapbook
A Dictionary	An Index
A Sketchbook	A Code Book
A Missal	A Notebook
A Guidebook	An Illuminated Book
A Pattern Book	A Pillow Book
An Album	A Cipher
A Crib	A Testament

Karl Young

2. Sample title for covers of big books--this part is usually done in black, with the title of the individual series between the end of the title with the author's name in a different color.

Since beginning the first two series of these books, I've been working on other series that explore the processes of bookmaking, the kinds of materials that can be used, the interaction of the strange and the familiar. A brief list of these follows:

THIRD SERIES — fat, shallow books: 2½'' across the spine; 8¼'' high x 7/8'' wide. Can be bent so that the front and back covers form a straight line and the text pages appear to form a semicircle when seen from top or bottom, and many pages can be seen simultaneously when looked at from the side opposite the spine. Of course, individual pages can be examined one at a time, too. Made of pages of multiply-printed scrap and clean-up sheets as in 1 & 2—other materials will be used later.

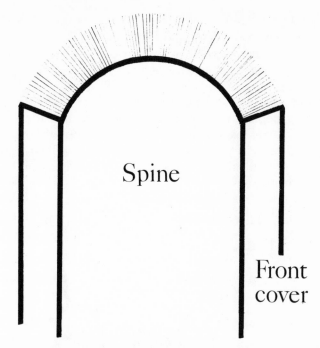

Spine

Front
cover

FOURTH SERIES: CUBES — same text sheets as in 1 & 2 but bound
so books' dimensions are 5" x 5" x 5". Will probably do some of
the following series in cube shapes eventually.

FIFTH SERIES: PORNOGRAPHY — pornographic pictures from
magazines, etc. bound on three sides—so you have to go to a great
deal of trouble to see any of the pages and can't see much even
when you do get a glimpse past an edge.

SIXTH SERIES — books whose pages are made from wooden two by
fours. Different texts for each of these, printed or written on
boards using various methods. These books can be used as musical
instruments by opening them and then closing them quickly. I'm
currently using one in performance of Jackson Mac Low's *Stanzas
for Iris Lezak.*

SEVENTH SERIES — books with glass mirrors for pages—you can
write your own texts in these with grease pencil (or any other similar medium) and then erase them whenever you wish.

EIGHTH SERIES — books made of reflective mylar—later books in
this series will have texts printed on mylar.

NINTH SERIES — see through books (actually, more like translucent
books when closed) made of clear acetate.

TENTH SERIES — books' pages made of used metal offset plates.
Not in the series but related: *A BOOK OF SOURCES AND DISAP-
PEARANCES* — paper money bound into covers with staples—have
so far just used one-dollar bills—if you use higher denominations,
you'll be more tempted to tear out leaves as you need them—so far

my problem has been never having enough spare money to make copies with, say, hundred-dollar bills.

Variations on the above: I'm currently in the process of making several books in series 1 & 4 for people whose work I've printed a lot of—these have something of each recipient's on each leaf (though not necessarily each page). One copy completed for Jerome Rothenberg, copies in progress for Toby Olson and Richard Kostelanetz. May not make any beyond these—or if I do, not many.

Some books in first, fifth, and sixth series will have two sets of pages—the subsidiary pages bound into wrap-around major pages. View from above:

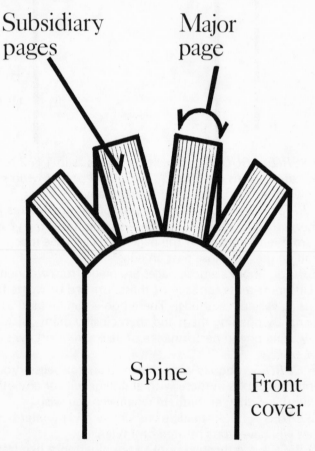

Subsidiary pages

Major page

Spine

Front cover

Notes: I wanted to include examples from series 1 in this essay, but given the facts that they're in different shades of gray, use multiple halftones, multiple colors, etc., they wouldn't reproduce decently. If you want some sample pages, send me two dollars within a year of the publication of this book and I'll send some along. (P.O. Box 11601—Shorewood/Milwaukee, Wisconsin/53211).

SOME REMARKS ON THE NOTION "VISUAL POETRY"

Eugen Gomringer

Writing is visible language. Thus, each written poem is a piece of language prepared for the sense-modality "sight." When concrete poetry developed the notion "visual-poetry" as well as that of "sound-poetry" or "audible-poetry," it intended to draw the attention to two important characteristics of the new conception of poetry. First, it should be pointed out that writing, seeing and reading on the one hand and listening-to-language on the other hand are two different medial fields—a fact that requires different experience and treatment for the making of poetry as well as for its reception-perception. Second, it should also be emphasized that both the seeing and reading of written poetry is heavily influenced by the manner in which anything written is preserved—be it in sand, on paper, with smoke or with any other medium. By introducing the notion "visual poetry," the medium-conscious concrete poet drew the attention to the artificiality of the "written" in every form. The notion of "visual poetry" focused anew our interest in traditional forms of singular signs (letters, punctuation marks, elementary symbols, signs for ciphers, etc.) as being "Gestalten" (figures?), in order to interpret them anew and to poetize them freshly, and also—as a forerunner of the so-called written painting!—to demonstrate in many examples the mental-motion process of writing and its realization in the shaping of writing.

Beside this physiological and psychic comprehension for the seeing and writing of poetry, concrete poetry set a high value on the philosophical notion of "identity." It tried especially by the many "ideograms," which originated in concrete poetry since the beginning, to create structures of language in which the meaning of signs and the shape of signs were identical, i.e. referred to one another mutually. This was valuable for singular signs as well as for super signs. Thus, e.g., the Spanish "y" in its meaning of "and" can be immediately seen and perceived as a sign for bi- or tri-partiteness. It is possible visually to link two or three signs in an additional manner, to bring them together in a perceptive-cognitive way. This meaning was given to this sign already by romantic symbolism. But then after several spatial systems of patterns in concrete poetry were established, the graphic-iconic element became more and more independent. Klaus Peter Dencker told me that already in my text "Kontur" ("Contour"), or even much earlier in my text "the black mystery is here," the iconic part was obvious as a separate quality. Claus Breuer finally published a book exemplifying the transition from the first phase of concrete poetry and its visual concept of written-language to a poetry with a universal repertoire of signs, which included special texts with dominating graphic patterns. This development to a kind of enigmatic picture-poetry, whose leading author in the German language is

Klaus Peter Dencker, is consequential, but it must be considered that in its mimetic tendency this is no longer a concrete poetry but rather an abstract one. The visual element in this picture-poetry is no longer based only on alphabetic signs, for very often it consists in collage-cum-constellations of mimetic signs and pure icons. This demonstration of "more world" by including disparate substrata must be seen without any doubt in relationship to a universal semiotic understanding of actual reality. This is not only a visual poetry—"visual" in connection with this poetry signifies only the visual-contact—but a *"semiotic poetry"*—presuming that such a new definition mostly represents illicit abbreviations and is made useful only by the vitality of the corresponding events.

Transcribed from a letter handwritten in English by the author, April, 1978.

FLOWCHARTING

Keith Rahmmings

1 *WHAT YOU SEE IS WHAT YOU GET*

visual poetry is a construction of concrete elements which become expressive in the process of synthesis and arrangement: the FORM of the work is in itself the CONTENT, and whatever expressiveness there is in the work ORIGINATES with the form. in visual poetry, the existence of an EXTERNAL mimetic component as objective referent is a NONESSENTIAL. WORDS or SYMBOLS need not relate in any way to concepts not linked directly to the kinetics of a piece. the SHAPE of a visual poem need fit into no relational contexts other than those central to the dynamics of the poem ITSELF. visual poetry may thus transcend REPRESENTATION, bypass POSSIBILITY and function ultimately as FACT.

2 *LANGUAGE A LA MODE*

the successful visual-language poem must center its immediacy of impact upon its visual aspects, for the immediate impact of it will be visual. language-centered visual constructs, regardless of their internal kinetics, will be viewed primarily as DESIGN and only secondarily as ANYTHING ELSE. this, however, in no way relegates the language-component of the visual-language poem to an INFERIOR status, for in the fact and act of composition all elements must function EF-FECTIVELY, INTERDEPENDENTLY, and, above all, ECONOMI-CALLY. stripped of its language-component, such work loses a large measure of its immediacy and dynamism, for the visual-language poem is neither design ALONE nor discrete concatonations of word/symbol but a syncretism of BOTH, deriving its impetus from their combined output. all components of a visual-language poem must function as mutual correlates; ultimately curving moebius-like back in and upon one another to become extensions and reflections of themselves.

3 *ADVERTIZEMENTS FOR MYSELF*

both PRINTOUTS and PLASTIC MATHEMATICS (available from Permanent Press, box 371, bklyn, 11230; $3.50 and $2.50 respectively, or exchange) are preoccupied with two fundamental concerns: ONE; the extension and elaboration of narrative modalities in language-centered visual constructs initiated in my previous book, ABRACADABRA, and TWO; the extension and elaboration of more adventurous and complex visual modalities as well as the INTER-FACING of both visual and narrative modalities to produce sequences and individual pieces which can exist simultaneously and effectively on multiple levels of perception/experience. the reader is

apprised that the operant techniques in any given piece may not be
immediately apparent. words, for example, may be grouped according to physical and morphological characteristics; imagistic and acous-
tic considerations; metric values; and so forth, but never, never, ran-
domly. sequences such as QWERTYUIOP and QWAD, for example,
contain effects-within-effects, such as acrostic structures concealing
other words and phrases. PRINTOUTS and PLASTIC MATHEMAT-
ICS should be approached by the reader/experiencer as albums containing multitrack recordings with different tracks proceeding at different rates of speed and levels of volume; tracks which may be perceived individually or on as many planes as perception admits.

Holly O'Grady

Sperry (1973), by John McClurg, has several definable characteristics of a novel: character development, a beginning, middle and end. More importantly, it has a wide range of invented visual motifs. Although some of the visual passages could be classified as illustrations, the unexpected inclusion of hand-stamped and collage elements challenge the reader's interpretative capacity to read both words and images simultaneously.

Words and images are used to form a literary polyphony. The verbal narrative forms one line of the polyphony while the drawings, photographs and other visual elements create related yet independent voices throughout the book. Thus, McClurg is able to overlap narratives keeping several story lines concurrent with each other.

McClurg printed the book on his own offset press controlling every facet of the production. (The edition is limited to 300.) Frequent use of direct paper masters, in contrast to standard offset plates, account for a freshness in printing which is easily mistaken for original drawings. Instead of being typeset, the text is largely handwritten. This reinforces the immediacy of the drawings and gives the book a tone of pronounced intimacy. Visually, the handwriting also constitutes a form of drawing. The handwriting varies somewhat according to each character reflecting McClurg's change in mood as he uses calligraphy to enhance each of the novel's dramatic episodes. Unlike medieval manuscripts where lettering sought a level of uniform consistency, the handwriting in *Sperry* becomes a seismograph to the author's energy, intensity and imagination.

McClurg's tripartite role as artist/writer/printer makes him a descendant in an uneven chain from William Blake. However, the content of McClurg's novel and his philosophical stance does not parallel the visionary Blake and his mythological cosmos. Although McClurg incorporates an allegory of King Midas into the novel, the story avoids mythologizing any of its characters in favor of an elevated melodrama.

The story, divided into four sections, is about the life of a grotesquely fat man, Sperry, and his eventual partnership with Tyrone, an "all-American" hustler and small-time money-schemer. Although Sperry and Tyrone are psychologically opposite—Sperry being introverted and empowered with perceptions into others, while Tyrone is extroverted, macho and adventurous—they both find a need to undertake first the risky enterprise of professional wrestling and then a traveling circus side-show.

The first section of the novel interweaves the allegory of King Midas with the story of Sperry's parents. The allegory is freely interpreted, dealing with the psychological transformation of the King as well as the gods removing the golden touch. The King who has ass's ears (by an earlier intervention from the gods as a punishment for not comply-

ing with their wishes) was ashamed of the ears until his release from
the touch. He finally and joyously makes public the fact that he has
ass's ears while symbolically shouting "He is as he appears." In *Sperry,*
this can be seen as well as read.

After King Midas, the theme of self-reconciliation is echoed throughout the book with Sperry's father, Dan, Sperry and finally Tyrone.
The juxtaposition of the King Midas allegory with the unfolding trag-
edy of Dan and his wife, Margaret, forms the first melodrama. Margaret believes that she has turned down a potential career as a tap
dancer and movie star to marry an obscure high school speech teacher. Over a period of time she becomes an alcoholic to ease the pain
of her unfulfilled life. Dan not only suffers from Margaret's drinking
and her gentlemen "friends," but also from being too short. He wears
elevator shoes and obsessively seeks remedies that will make him taller.

In the most emotional scene in this section Margaret, who has
learned that she has a terminal illness, gives herself a going away party.
Late that night she goes into her bedroom and through alcoholic
carelessness sets the bedroom on fire and dies. The scene is effectively
dramatized by a singular example of handwriting as drawing. Dan, unable to rescue Margaret stands on the other side of the door lamenting
for her forgiveness. On two facing pages the father's voice is depicted
by awkward and tormented writing which becomes almost illegible
and finally dissolves at the end of the second page into a thin black
rectangle and then a larger black rectangle—a void of despair, i.e., language becomes a pure abstract symbol.

The second section describes Sperry's life after Dan has died of a
heart attack. The use of description particularly in Sperry's eating
habits is precise and sounds almost clinical. As if to underscore that
description an actual wrapper from a Hersey candy bar is collaged onto one of the pages which also includes drawings of eggs, bacon, malts,
hamburgers and Fritoes. The use of this wrapper suddenly makes the
description of food more than a mere recital of what a fat man eats.
In a way it is hard to be critical of Sperry's incredible overeating,
when one is so directly confronted with a contemporary symbol of
temptation.

Sperry frequently promises to go on a diet, a vow that is as often
as not precipitated by some terrible humiliation suffered because of
his obesity. Children, at times capable of great cruelty, not only as-
sail Sperry with verbal abuse but also inflict physical pain on him. Believing that someone with all that fat could not feel pain, Sperry is
punched, poked and at one point someone even puts a metal spring
clamp on his butt. Thus, Sperry finds himself in the hospital.

Sperry's moment of reconciliation grows out of a number of traumas suffered in his brief overnight stay at the hospital: the doctor
putting in the stitches exposes Sperry's big bottom for an unneces-
sarily long time, his roommate makes fun of him, and for the first
time in his life he throws up, attracting even more attention to himself. Emotionally exhausted by these ordeals, Sperry prays for

death. He awakens in the morning disappointed at still being alive but having survived these traumas he receives, as such gifts are granted, inexplicably, the power to bless people. It is through this power that a reconciliation comes about between his formidable exterior and his patient, empathetic nature. Because of his insight and his capacity to bless people, he becomes at the end of his rather short life more than just a circus fat man. He becomes a spiritual curiosity; but the author, carefully, does not elevate him into a religious oddity, saint or faith healer. His spiritual effect helps people transcend their own revulsion to see Sperry not as he appears but as he really is.

The visual motifs which accompany this moment of crisis in the hospital again use visual abstraction as a literary symbol. Juxtaposed over the text, on two facing pages, is the repetition of a hand-stamped image of the underside of a man's shoe and trouser cuff. The text relates his wish to die. The placement of the image is rhythmical and relentless, and it echoes Sperry's view of himself as a victim. The next two facing pages are empty of words—two gray rectangles implying a state of spiritual passivity—are not like the black rectangles mentioned before, which are portrayed as literally growing out of Dan's grief and anguish. The last two facing pages in this sequence return the verbal narrative. Words occupy the extreme left-hand margin and bottom leaving a large white rectangular space in the center of the page. The page opposite has no words; it has only a glaring yellow rectangle appearing all the brighter since it is surrounded by a generous white border. As a sign of inevitable daylight, the yellow rectangle is in some ways as relentless as the hand-stamped image of the foot. Only in this case, it amplifies Sperry's victory in resolving his own internal conflicts.

Sections III and IV are both shorter and faster-paced. Section III describes Tyrone's life more through his adventures than through the pathetic confrontations found in the previous sections. A typewritten surrealist section about a bill collector (the only typed passage) shares a series of pages with poems and straight verbal narrative about Tyrone's early life. The bill collector story reveals the most unsavory aspect of Tyrone's character by underscoring the least palatable role in making money—that of having to collect it. However, Tyrone is ruthless in his attempts to acquire money without a trace of remorse or mercy. As a result his financial endeavors often end in emotional and physical peril for others. For example, he takes revenge on one of his former employers (not without some justification) causing him to loose his nerve, his business and then his life.

The side of Tyrone that is calculating and unfeeling is shown in scattered drawings of the Frankenstein monster—an image of his alter ego. Even visually more startling are two children's drawings (contributed by McClurg's son, Joram) showing a child squirting another child in the ear. As previously mentioned, the cruelty of children to each other is portrayed as severe, and in Tyrone's case it is a condition he never outgrows until his more mature adult years—the end of the novel. Tyrone, interestingly, does not appear as a monster to those who see only the conventional good looks of a fifties American crew-cut hero.

Other visual motifs in this section focus on illustrating Tyrone's careers first in roller-skating shows and then in the circus world with Sperry. The use of photographs from forties roller-skating shows as well as the inclusion of documents such as a receipt from the Plaza Hotel in Milwaukee emphasize the shift in the book from a more internal struggle to external encounters with the world.

The extensive display of visual motifs and their interaction with the narrative has only been touched upon here. The influences on McClurg include everything from underground comics, as in certain passages on Tyrone, to minimalism, as pages of minimal images dealing with Sperry's crisis. One drawing in particular, however, presents itself as an embodiment of the visual/verbal novel. The first drawing and the first page of the book shows King Midas looking in a mirror. Instead of seeing his reflection, the King sees the image of Sperry.

Outside the context of the novel the drawing might be viewed as a rather tongue-in-cheek reference to Picasso's "Woman in the Mirror." Certainly the linear strength of McClurg's drawing would make the analogy meaningful. The drawing, however, like the written King Midas allegory, parallels the structure of the novel. By positioning the drawing at the beginning of the book, McClurg alerts the reader to the relevance of the visual/verbal allegory which will follow, as well as the polysemous nature of the total object. On one level it has highly narrative implications. The point at which King Midas accepts his ass's ears is the moment he has survived the affliction of his golden touch and regained his long lost use of normal human emotions. The King can compassionately look at the image of an innocent, spiritual Sperry who is also a literal embodiment of certain human frailties.

On a more provocative level, the drawing can be viewed as a means of expressing duality. It is a symbolic portrayal of one self rather than two. This is not meant to imply that Sperry is King Midas but rather that the two images create a more complete dialog in the ongoing conflict between good and evil. It is interesting to note that it is Tyrone who finally acquires the ass's ears at the end of the novel, thus uniting the partnership of Tyrone and Sperry.

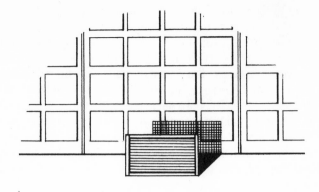

WHY IS THIS BOOK DIFFERENT FROM ALL OTHER BOOKS?

Paul Zelevansky

As we progress, the astute reader will notice in this foreword a familiar tone that reflects the spirit, if not the letter of an earlier hand that wrote, with astonishing beauty, a tale about a man entranced on a mountain.

We will begin by saying, with provocation in mind, that our story concerns a mountain that sat upon a man. It was of course not a material, geologic mountain that sat upon this man, although such piles are incorporated in other mythologies, and mounds on the earth will have a place in the plot later on. We are talking now of an idea mountain, or better yet, an ideal mountain that develops and erodes, appears and disappears before our eyes. As with the juggler, one hand builds while the other takes away.

So it is the idea of this mountain △ (pay close attention at this early stage, for the work and the mountain are already upon you) that sat upon this man. Long before, when this notion was first felt, his sense of weight was a provocation to his sense of balance, and the man, soon to become the narrator, spent ages on one foot considering whether the pain was holding up the pleasure, or the pleasure holding up the pain. Not to mention that he liked the replacement even less than the original (half empty, half full) and why was he lending his support to the question in the first place? As in times before, the weight prevailed, in fact it grew mythical in proportion to the everyday, and the man, soon to become the Author, set out to create its

---

The foreword from *The Case for the Burial of Ancestors,* a visual novel by Paul Zelevansky.

mass, piece by piece, upon the whiteness of the page. And so an epic heart began to beat within the mountain.

As we progress, the astute viewer will notice a familiar slant to this building, that reflects the spirit, if not the law of a continually ingesting purpose, which is to fill the endless space and surface of the page with wonder and life. To accumulate and pile association, vision and memory; to construct, with lightness, strength and clarity, an enviable Babel in the air of all we look upon. We speak, we listen, we peer around, we pass through, we hide behind, we hover above, we touch with our fingers, we follow with our eyes, we cross the space of the known world even to the rim of the city; we receive, we dangle our feet in the river. In short, we inhabit the space, and by extension, place the reader's feet within the plot.

We ask you to accept the edges of the page, as you accept the proscenium which contains the play. Both are places of action, vessels of history, and time passes within at its own measured pace. It is important to remember that we may pass freely in or out of the space, for the screen is porous between us. The proscenium is no less an arch and a portal than a frame for our sight.

And do not forget that you are holding a book in your hands, and must adjust the scale accordingly. If your image or your name was set before you, it could walk the page with abandon, while you sat there in your chair. Is it not a wonder that we can build or destroy such boundaries at our whim?

If we suspend our judgment and our clocks within the theater, let us be no less generous—or impatient—here. It is wise to remember, and you will hear this again, that one best receives this notion of foundation while sitting quietly and waiting for the moment to arrive.

Consider another form of the slant to this body: one that reflects the spirit, if not the line of a continually reflecting surface. This slant is found in the cross-hatching of the page with lines ▨▨▨ for the plain purpose of casting shadows on the ground. Whether to solidify the floor, to establish a wall in the air, to identify the direction of the light, or to remind us of an unseen presence, it is a marker that coordinates our position. You, the reader, are also present on this screen, by implication. It is a gift set down before an audience of one.

Why is this book different from all other books? If explanation is still necessary, (remember the building of the tale is already upon you) we will continue with a discussion of the pieces, which are given and taken away in turn. (Those who need no more convincing should nonetheless be patient and tolerant of the others. At all other times we call the roll, but on this occasion we welcome strangers. So, you may sit back, but remain watchful of the proceedings. The space above the book contains both enchantment and exile.)

To the pieces: Speak of the exchange between word and image. Consider the gradations, progressions and comparisons. Picture the labyrinth of connection drawn between this and that, dark and light, positive and negative, thick and thin, up and down, rough and smooth, long and short, near and far, in and out, backwards and forwards, off and on, gathering and unfolding, loud and soft, beginning and ending, shadow and substance—when, within our book, past, present, and potential exist at once. Internal, external, above and below, projection and echo exist within the same geography. Where all are visible, all are manifest, all are simultaneous in thought. Words are within pictures, pictures are within words, and both speak of each other, together and apart. Out of the exchange comes the vehicle and the form: the screen of projection, the floor of reflection, the surface, the page.

All of which would induce confusion, an anvil chorus of static noise and conflicting cues, if it were played out at one time, without modulation. That would be more than anyone should have to contend with between the covers of a book. So, although the story is indeed upon you, do not fear to be crushed by it. Most of the web is beneath the surface, hairlike and light without a trace. The full, cacophonic view is opened only rarely.

But tastes and fragments of the whole picture rise frequently. They hang upon the original frame like notes clustered on a staff. In motion they pass along channels, paths, tracks and boundaries. As destinations and markers they measure distances. As signs and symbols scaled down on maps they plot the course. As characters and inhabitants they move with gesture and rhythm. As thoughts they grow, they diminish, getting smaller, lighter, fainter, further away, light enough and small enough to be airmailed, unseen to a later page. Time passes, weather shifts, days turn from dark to light. All is recorded on calendars and clocks, diaries and logs, and replayed; every shift across every field. Around the borders, along the margins, between the lines where we sit, at the beginning beneath this mountain of an idea.

All of which would be floating debris, spouting lava, and shifting sand, without some skin to contain it. A story will hold the descriptive, the metaphorical, and the kinetic in equation and so supply us with a base for entertainment.

To begin. We will present a History, a story of time and travel, born of the vision, sign and look of the man beneath the mountain—a story of search, discovery, study and fabrication, whose truths hang with implied purpose like grapes on the vine.

The History will be divided into two books. Book I. will encompass all significant myths, tales, accumulations, interventions and moments of generation that led to the foundation of the H Tabernacle and the beginning of the golden age of Hegemonian culture. Book II. will describe the physical construction of the Tabernacle, the course of observance and ritual, and the ultimate effect of Hegemonian sovereignty on the known world at that time. This will be the story of a people whose time had come. Who saw their implied purpose and were ready to squeeze it. What follows will be a record of the moves, combinations and decisions available to the players involved.

The tale will span from A through H within the known alphabet: from ARRIVAL to BACKGROUND to COLD FACTS to DUST to EXILE to FOOTSTEPS to GOD to HISTORY and around again. That which hides on the other side of H, called next in the line of ascent, is beyond the understanding of the players involved, though they move towards it with the complete assurance that something is there. They are a collective lot who speak mainly through the formal We. As their concerns are adjusted to their needs, they are sure of their place and sit well upon the seat of contentment. Are they blind, or eminently flexible?

The tale ends where it begins. History is the vessel that makes the voyage. It carries within its hold the resolution of the frame.

We are nearing the end of the foreword. It is the time to reveal the face behind the narrative voice. At this point we can dispense with the man beneath the mountain. He is no more than an allusion, a figure of speech, and his weight can now be lifted from us. Others will take on the burden of the narrative. (Once Brothers, we now may may pass for Others) Joining with myself, for the moment, is the voice of the Puppeteer. Atop, alone, sitting before the green felt of the gaming table, the Puppeteer watches over the proceedings without passion. For the Hegemonians and their forebears the Puppeteer was the embodiment of their need for guidance and clarity on the Way. When they looked up to the Heavens it was the Puppeteer that they sought. Proof of their implied purpose was made visible to their sight. For they saw the face of the Puppeteer cast down upon the Nation.

The voice you now hear will stand in for many in the composite. For the words of this mouth are words of construction, which leave marks in abundant form for those who might hear.

All things said and meant will spin like a top.

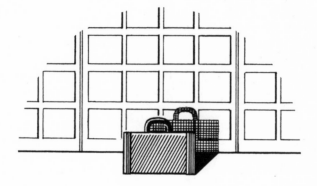

ART AUTOBIOGRAPHY (1978)

Richard Kostelanetz

Towards the end of his career, Moholy-Nagy described the pur-
pose of a retrospective exhibition as that of making the spectator
'travel' as far as he had travelled himself, and added, 'What a long
way to go!' —Frank Popper, Art-Action and Participation *(1975).*

The thought of doing my own visual poetry initially came to me
while bored with Antonioni's *Blow-Up* early in July, 1967. The next
day, I wrote—rather *drew*—my first poem, "Tributes to Henry Ford,"
using rulers, French curves and stencils that I purchased at a neighborhood store; and the fact that this five-image poem remains among my
most reprinted, most familiar works both pleases and depresses me. I
had already seen some visual poetry, initially at London's Institute
for Contemporary Art two years before and again in the then-current
"concrete" issue of the *Chicago Review.* Even though most of the
work collected under that "concrete" label did not particularly appeal to me, I thought that the idea of casting language in an alternative visual form was profoundly suggestive.

Much of the glorious summer of 1967, just after my twenty-seventh
birthday, was spent working with my new art, producing many pieces
that have since become more familiar—"Disintegration," "Echo,"
"Nymphomania," and the "Football Forms," among others. Some
of these early works are explicitly mimetic, my drawing enhancing
the words in representational ways; for my aim then was the creation
of a visual form so appropriate to a certain word that the whole would
make an indelible impact—an afterimage that would be implanted in
the viewer's mind, primarily because the shape endowed the word
with an incipiently mythic resonance. Though limited by a lack of
artistic training, I nonetheless felt obliged to do all the drawing myself; since my works were poetry, rather than commercial design, I
decided that they should not hide the idiosyncracies of my own hand.

Toward the end of that summer, I discovered the technology of
photostatting and then began to submit my work to periodical edi-
tors I knew, mostly because they had published essays of mine; but
nearly all of them were unresponsive, some even suggesting that I was
wasting my time with this poetry. My initial acceptance came from
Paul Carroll, who was then editing his pioneering anthology, *The*
Young American Poets (1968); and my appearance there served the
crucial professional function of certifying, in my own mind at least,
my status as "a poet" as well as "a critic." To celebrate the publication of his anthology, Carroll sponsored a series of "readings" in New
York; and in response to his invitation to participate, I developed the

presentational form I still use—"an illuminated demonstration," in which a carousel projector throws my visual poems up on a screen, while I, their author, standing behind the audience, declaim a non-synchronous, voice-over narration that is filled not with specific explanations but general concepts that the audience may or may not choose to relate to what they see. A decade ago, I had only enough slides to fill a single carousel tray; now I can fill several and often project two different sets of images simultaneously.

Since a book's worth of poems existed almost from the beginning, I decided, early in 1968, to dedicate the volume to my most inventive teacher at college, S. Foster Damon, and even announced the dedication that February at Foster's 75th birthday party. Copies of my initial collection were submitted to several publishers, some of whom had previously issued my books; none of them took it. By 1970 I reluctantly recognized that commercial publishers in America were not yet hospitable to visual poetry. (Several years later, none of them have yet matured that far.) It was thus inevitable that *Visual Language* should be published under the imprint of Assembling Press, which I had cofounded that summer; and in printing the book, I had two ulterior motives in mind: I wanted to see this work reviewed (it wasn't) and I needed sufficient copies to distribute to anthologists and friends. Photostats were becoming an unnecessary nuisance and expense.

The publication of *Visual Language* also forced me to consider alternative ways of making nonsyntactic visual poetry. I tried to make a complete visual alphabet, parts of which are reprinted in my second collection, *I Articulations* (1974); I also compiled collections of synonyms that were then visually enhanced, such as the "Live-Kill" pair (1972). Another new development, begun in 1970, is the handwritten visual poem, such as "The East Village" (1970-71). Here I wanted to get away from the centered space and single perceptual perspective of my earlier work. Since I am scarcely able to invent a situation from scratch—or, to be more precise, since I am more inventive with materials than imaginative with situations—I chose a familiar subject: the neighborhood in which I then lived. As my theme was the variousness of the individual side streets, each of which has its own characteristic spatial qualities, its own details and its own sounds, I did a one-page portrait in language and space for each block. I thought of hiring a professional calligrapher to redo my peculiar handwriting, but the single sample I saw reminded me too much of the rigors of linotype. And *that* was precisely what I was trying to avoid. So, once again, the best solution was letting the work reveal my own hand. I originally wanted Assembling Press to publish *The East Village* as a single book, on large 11" x 17" pages. However, since twelve images seemed insufficient for a book, even in such a large format, I eventually incorporated the work into the 7" x 10" pages of *I Articulations.* Instead, a later, longer handwritten poem, "Portraits from Memory," appeared as an entire 35-page book (1975), in which each page contains a verbal-visual portrait of a woman I might have known. Here, as elsewhere in my work, the titles of individual pieces tend to be rather explicit.

I had always thought that my best visual poems should be available in enlarged forms, not only to make them available for gallery exhibition but also to enhance their afterimage capabilities. Back in 1970, I made a large photostat of "Concentric" for a two-man exhibition. In the summer of 1974, I took a silkscreening course which resulted in a few enlarged prints; but since my technical competence was limited, in the following year I commissioned the printmaker Stephen Procuniar to make *Word Prints,* a set of seven, 26" x 40". By 1976, I got into photolinens, with images even larger than the prints, and had them stretched, much like paintings, over wooden bars. I still enjoy visual poetry more than the movies.

II

Probably from the time I began to read I had an ambition to write fiction; but everything I drafted between my freshman year of college and early 1968 eventually struck me as an obvious echo of some text I already admired. At least seven times I began a novel that, upon close inspection, was clearly an imitation of Nathanael West's great work, *The Day of the Locust;* and so this ambition subsided, along with my dreams of becoming a professional football player or a rock musician. I felt no need to recapitulate what had already been written, and did not know how to write what had not.

In doing poetry, I had already discovered the idea of a constraint so severe that it would prevent me from using language in familiar forms; and that primary restriction was the use of only one word that would then be visually enhanced. An imposed constraint, I discovered, serves to force the creative imagination to resist convention, if not cliché; and like meter in traditional poetry, the constraint I chose also encourages puzzle-solving and other forms of playfulness. This approach struck me as rather useful at generating original work; and perhaps the easiest measure of the difference or newness of my work is whether or not the reader feels challenged to discern sense and significance in what at first seems inscrutable.

Early in 1968, I began to think about a similar kind of severe constraint for writing fiction; and after a few abortive experiments, I hit upon the hypothesis of writing a story with no more than two words to a paragraph; and for a subject, I chose the conveniently familiar one of boy meets girl. This plot appears frequently in my fiction, not because I have anything particularly profound to say about heterosexual encounters, but because a familiar, transparent subject makes both myself and my readers more aware of the technical issues that really interest me. Once the two-word paragraphs of "One Night Stood" were drafted, I typed them out, indenting alternative lines; and the following winter I realized that each two-word phrase could take up the entire page of a book, thereby expanding the story into a minimal novel (that was not published until 1977). Subsequent verbal fictions are similarly skeletal—"Excelsior," with only one word to a paragraph; "Milestones in a Life," in which chronological numbers are followed by just a single word or sometimes two; and "Dialogue," which is composed of only two words, "Yes" and "No," repeated in different ways. One attractive result of these technical departures is a fluid, indefinite sense of fictional space and time.

That summer of 1969, I discovered how to make visual fiction, realizing an implication of my much-reprinted "Football Forms"— that images in sequence could tell a story, whose temporal rhythm is based upon the time a typical reader takes to turn the page; and that perception informed not only my alphabet novella, *In the Beginning* (1971), but also my initial abstract fictions—those consisting only of lines, lacking words, save for their titles. That summer I also drafted the theoretical statement, "Twenty-five Fictional Hypotheses," that even several years later is still reprinted for its radical possibilities. It suggests, among other things, that anything can be used to tell a story, not only nonsyntactic language but visual materials as well; and of course I practiced what I preached. I also noticed a crucial difference between poetry and fiction: Whereas the former tends to concentrate both image and effect, fiction creates a world of related activity.

A further development in my story-telling is the work composed of sequential four-sided symmetrical line-drawings that metamorphose in systemic sequence. Begun in 1974, these "Constructivist Fictions," as I call them, presently include not only two published collections of short fiction, *Constructs* (1974) and *Constructs Two* (1978), but two more unpublished collections, in addition to two full-length novels, *Symmetries* (1979) and *Intermix* (unpublished). A variation of this Constructivist theme is *And So Forth* (also unpublished), in which the geometric images, by contrast, are *not* perfect symmetries, and their order is *not* fixed.

In the summer of 1970, I drafted another verbal fiction, entitled *Openings & Closings,* which remains, in one crucial respect, the most conventional imaginative piece I have ever written—it contains full sentences! Nonetheless, it resembles my other verbal fictions in observing a truncating constraint; for whereas the earlier stories had one or two words to a paragraph, here I decided to suggest, within single sentences, either a story that might follow or one that could have gone before. The isolated sentences were literally either the openings

(of hypothetically subsequent stories) or the closings (of hypothetically previous stories). These could be considered incomplete stories,
it is true; yet it was my aim to make a single sentence be artistically
sufficient (and let readers imagine the rest). As there is no internal
connection between any particular opening or any closing, I thought
from the beginning that the stories should best be set in two different
styles of type—italics for the openings, roman for the closings—with
plenty of white space between them; but not until 1975 was *Openings and Closings* published. Invited, in 1976, to exhibit this work in
a gallery, I typed the sentences out on individual cards—one card to
a sentence—again using italics for the openings and roman for the
closings. These cards were then scattered, in no particular order, initially over a display board and later around the gallery's walls. I like
this work for its leaps in space and the changes of its voice and tones,
from item to adjacent item; but I doubt if I could ever again do a fiction that was so dependent on conventional expository sentences.

III

In my first numerical work, "Accounting," drafted early in 1969, I
wanted to see if numbers could be used in lieu of words or letters; and
that numerical piece was also the first of its kind to appear in print,
initially in my anthology *Future's Fictions* (1971) and then as a separate booklet (1973). The profession of accounting, like this numerical
piece, documents processes of accumulation; but not until 1972,
when preparing a revised version for chapbook publication, did I realize that this incremental sequence should end, like an accountant's
tabulation, with a row of zeroes. That new numerical conclusion
gave the narrative an ironic twist that, in my judgment, enhanced the
work considerably. *Accounting* visually resembles my novella *In the
Beginning,* composed around the same time; but whereas the former
comes to a definite end, the final page of the latter suggests that the
narrative could continue forever. That diametric difference in their
sequential form indicates, of course, comparable differences in meaning.

Late in 1972, I set everything else aside to see how far I could take
my growing interest in numbers—to see whether I could create a Literature composed of numbers alone. I thought at the time that I was
making a book of "poems and stories," remembering my earlier distinction. However, by the following year, I realized that these works
were actually becoming something else—a "numerature," perhaps; a
"numerical art," to be sure. My aim in working with numbers was no
longer the writing of poems and stories but the creation of a numerical
field that is both visually and numerically coherent, with varying degrees of visual-numerical complexity. These works do not merely incorporate numerals within visual concerns, like, say, certain Jasper

Johns paintings; my pieces are literally about the language of numbers.
A principal difficulty in communicating this work, I belatedly discovered, is that audiences must be *numerate* to comprehend them, much
as they must be *literate* to read modernist poetry and fiction.

My initial arrangements were numerically simple. "1024," for instance, incorporates both the parts and the factors of that variously
divisible number, while "Indivisibles" is a field of visually unrelated
numbers whose common property is that nothing can be divided into
any of them (except, of course, themselves and one). As before, titles
in my works tend to be explicit. Realizing that my aim was arithmeti-
cal patterns that could, like art (and unlike puzzles), be numerically
appreciated again and again, I then tried to create numerical fields
whose relationships were more multiple and less obvious. In works
like the diamond-shaped "Parallel Intervals," I began, I think, to approach the levels of complexity that I admire in serial music and *Fin-
negans Wake,* for numbers were more conducive than words for my
penchants for rigorous systems, structural complexity and geometric
order. (Simply because one number can go next to any other number,
numerical syntax, unlike that of words, is also infinitely permissible.)
In addition, these number pieces realize an empirical ideal that,
though esthetically heretical, has long haunted me—that all the artistic activity that one identified in the work could be *verified* by another
observer and yet be rich enough to be appreciated again and again. My
first numerical prints were done in 1974 and the first numerical photolinens in 1976.

IV

In the spring of 1974, I completed *Recyclings,* the third and most
successful of my first series of experiments with continuous nonsyn-
tactical prose. *Recyclings* was made by subjecting earlier essays of
mine to selective processes that destroyed their original syntax, while
retaining their characteristic language. The pages of *Recyclings* can
thus be read both horizontally, like normal prose, or vertically, as the
eyes, moving down and around the page, can perceive not only consis-
tencies in diction but repeated words that usually indicate an identifiable ulterior source or subject.

Considering how to declaim this work aloud, I hit upon a structure
that could aurally incorporate both the horizontal and the vertical—re-
cruiting a chorus of readers each of whom would speak the text horizontally, one word after the other; but rather than read in unison,
each new reader would declaim from the opening word, beginning to
speak approximately one line behind his or her predecessor. Since I
was not aiming for any specific vertical juxtapositions, but constant
vertical relationships, each reader could go at his own pace, and in his
own manner. I assumed that an audience listening carefully would

hear vertical relationships—words spoken simultaneously, much like chords in music—amid the horizontal polyphonic declamation.

When invited to be a guest artist at the new radio studios of WXXI-FM, Rochester, N.Y., March, 1975, I realized a seven-track version in which all the declamatory voices are my own, each one amplified differently from the others. Although it was my initial intention to realize aurally certain qualities that were visually present in *Recyclings,* I found that the experience of listening to this audiotape is really quite different. This is not poetic declamation, as we customarily know it, but something closer to the performance of a musical score, probably because it mixes a language text with compositional structures more typical of music. Though "sound poetry" to some and "text-sound" to others, I prefer to classify this particular audiopiece as "sound prose," because the initial material is not poetry but prose.

My other initial audiotapes are largely straight declamations of my truncated stories, amplified and enhanced in various, comparatively modest ways. For *Openings & Closings,* I put the opening sentences on one side of a stereo stystem, and the closing sentences on the other; and in *Foreshortenings,* a later verbal fiction, a voice clearly identifiable as mine swaps single-sentence lines with a chorus of my voice, both sides repeating the same repertoire of eighty-four simple sentences in increasingly different ways. (The principal reason why my own voice takes both sides of this and other audio conversations is that most of my tapes were done late at night, with only an engineer and myself in the studio. And someone else had to watch the voice levels on the recording machines!)

Since 1976, I have favored familiar religious and political texts, such as the Declaration of Independence or the Lord's Prayer, electronically modified in ways that make them aurally incomprehensible to most ears, were not the texts already familiar. Indeed, religious materials strike me as especially suitable for electronic enhancement, which generally increases the suggestion of sacredness. Sometime after completing the initial recording of "Praying to the Lord," where a single voice speaking a familiar text is electronically multiplied into a vibrantly cacaphonous chorus, I came across R. Murray Schafer's observation, in *The Tuning of the World* (1977): "It was not until the Renaissance that God became portraiture. Previously He had been conceived as sound or vibration." In the back of my mind, when I began this piece, was the experience, the previous summer, of seeing the valley to the west of Mount Sinai, and then imagining the presence of thousands of noisy Israelites waiting for Moses to return. Vibration, I now thought, could also be interpreted as the sound of the multitudes venerating God. Schaefer's remark also reminds me of Marshall McLuhan's observation that electronic media of communication recreate the sensory experience of preprint peoples.

The main distinguishing characteristics of my audiotapes so far have been the use of inventive, uncommon language structures, whether truncated lines or nonsyntactic prose, and then the realization of aural experiences that would be unfeasible, if not impossible, in live performance. It makes no sense for me or anyone to do in one medium something that could be done better in another.

V

Late in 1975, I was invited to be guest artist at the Synapse Studio of Syracuse University. Here I worked not with a single engineer-producer, as at WXXI-FM, but with an institutional staff of young instructors, graduate assistants and undergraduates. With their help, I realized video versions of four earlier texts. To do "Excelsior," a truncated story in which two people make love in one-word paragraphs, I created a circular visual image for each character. As voices change, the screen flashes rapidly from one moving image to the other. In "Plateaux," with its single-word paragraphs, each relating a different stage (or plateau) in the development of a love affair, we used video feedback to create a kaleidoscopic moiré pattern that changes slowly in no particular direction, complementing visually the pointless, circular development of the fiction's plot. For *Openings & Closings,* I instructed the large staff, first, to alternate between color cameras for the openings and black and white cameras for the closings, and then to make each new image (mostly of me reading) as different as possible from the one before, thus realizing visually the leaps of time and space that characterize the radically discontinuous prose text. Finally, whereas the audio *Recyclings* has nonsyntactic prose read by nonsynchronous voices (all mine), for the color video I hit upon the image of pairs of speaking lips (all mine again)—one pair of lips for the first "Recycling," two pairs for the second, etc. We went up to eight pairs of lips in the studio; however, one-inch videotape that has been passed, or superimposed, eight times has an electronically weak signal, so not only were the last two generations lost completely, but the next two (counting backwards) had to be reshot in black and white to survive on tape. Were *Recyclings* to be redone in a professional quad (two-inch tape) studio, all the images would have a much surer chance of surviving in their optimal form.

In 1977, long frustrated in my desire to work only with the sophisticated video equipment necessary for my technologically complex ideas, I began to think about working with the more limited possibilities of ½" or ¾" videotape. Most of the pieces I made in this format exploit a contrast between words that are heard and facial images that are seen, the camera's close-up eye assimilating only part of the speaking figure. I also used the character-generator to put directly on the screen visible words that would either enhance or counterpoint the

language spoken on the tape. Again, it was my aim to create not doc-
umentations of live performances or dramatizations of stories—both
current fashions in video art—but works based on language that could
exist only on videotape, because they exploited the unique potentialities of the medium.

In 1976, I began to work with film, initially as an informal guest in
a graduate animation course. With Barton Weiss, I made films composed entirely of words, which thus must be *read,* quite rapidly, in order to be "seen." The common joke is that these silent movies are
"all titles, no action." What makes such entirely verbal films interesting to me are two complementary phenomena: the inordinate concentration of the viewers, who realize that they must pay constant, strict
attention if they are to see everything, and then the experience of
reading,in unison, with a crowd of strangers, in contrast to the conventional experience of reading a text of one's own choosing, at one's
own speed, by oneself. The second set of films, made in collaboration with Peter Longauer, shoot the Constructivist Fictions in negative, so that four-sided symmetries of white lines appear on the black
screen, in sequences that are systematically composed (complementing the systemic composition of the drawings). Of all the media in
which I have worked, film requires the most laboring time and seems,
in terms of what I would ultimately like to do with it, the least developed.

In the summer of 1977, I finally completed photographs worth
preserving. I had been thinking about the art of photography ever
since doing my documentary monograph on *Moholy-Nagy* (1970), for
the example of Moholy taught me not only that I could work in several arts at once but that, if I did photography, I should create images
that could exist only as photographs—that would not be "moments"
from films, say, or extensions of documentary reportage. After several abortive experiments, I hit upon the idea of taking a single 8" x
10" photograph of myself, cutting it apart into eighty equally sized
squares, and then recomposing these squares into eighty new pictures
which I called *Reincarnations.* Given my recent ambivalent feelings
about exact systems, the geometric rearrangements of these photographs are only roughly, or incompletely, systemic, while the order of
the images is not fixed. (The analogue in my Constructivist Fiction is
And So Forth, which was done around the same time.) For a second
sequential piece, completed in 1978 and tentatively called *Recall,*
each of the photographs is recomposed within scrupulously systemic
principles, and the order of the pictures is fixed. At the time that examples of *Reincarnations* first appeared in print, I did not own a camera and never had; but one theme of this Moholyan memoir is that
the lack of such prerequisites, let alone "education," should never
prevent me, or anyone else, from working in any art. Sometime soon,

I hope to get into holography, once again importing previous concerns into new terrain, initially to see what might result, but finally to produce works of consequential art.

VI

Books both authored and designed by me have been appearing since 1970, when *Visual Language* was published; and an interest in alternative forms of bookmaking goes back to critical essays I published in 1968 and 1969. Not until 1975, however, did I realize that Book Art as such was a conscious creative concern of mine, and I immediately produced a set of volumes that explore alternative book forms—the accordion books, *Modulations* and *Extrapolate;* the handwritten book, *Portraits from Memory;* a chapbook with horizontal images spread over two open pages, *Come Here;* and then the cardbook, *Rain Rains Rain* (1976); a book that exists only on audiotape, *Experimental Prose* (1976); the two-front book, *Prunings/Accruings* (1977) and the two newsprint books, *Numbers: Poems & Stories* (1976) and *One Night Stood* (1977). That last title, *One Night Stood,* also appeared as a small paperback book, 4" x 5 3/8"; for the existence of both editions creates the illustrative contrast of reading the same verbal text of two-word paragraphs in two radically different book forms. That is, not until one reads both books together will he or she realize how perceptibly different the two formats can be.

VII

In my creative work so far, there has been a continuing concern with alternative materials for traditional genres, such as poetry and fiction, and then with alternative media, such as audio and video, which sometimes enhance the preexisting materials and other times function as a willful constraint. Predisposed to invention, I had intended from the beginning to make imaginative works that looked and "read" like nothing else anyone knew; and since my reasons for making art were quite different from those behind my critical essays, separate fundamental concerns insured that my professional functions were not confused. In doing things differently, I have accepted the likelihood of losses with the gains; and should people complain, as they sometimes do, that certain qualities they like in my criticism are absent from this creative work, my reply is that the latter stems from different purposes in myself and hopefully exhibits certain qualities absent from my criticism. "In contemporary art," Moholy-Nagy once wrote, "often the most valuable part is not that which presents something new, but that which is missing. In other words, the spectator's delight may be derived partly from the artist's effort to eliminate the obsolete solutions of their predecessors."

Though superficially diverse, not only in media but styles, my crea-

tive works still exhibit certain unifying qualities, such as riskiness, rig-
or, clarity, structural explicitness, variousness, empiricism, and conceptual audacity—qualities that might also characterize my critical
writing, perhaps because they define my personal temper (and are
thus as close as the work can be to being me); and my creative concern with innovative structure is also a principal theme of my criticism and anthologies. Two goals in mind for both my art and my criticism are that they be more complex and yet more accessible, if
only to prove that these aims need not be contradictory.

All my creative work can also be seen as the dialectical result of pit-
ting my traditional education and professional experience (with expository writing) against my antithetical effort to transcend conventional forms—to write a poetry of intentionally limited language, to
make a fiction exclusively of lines, to compose with numbers, to mul-
ti-track declaimed language, etc. Since much of the work involves a
mixing of materials, the process of perceiving it customarily combines
at least two perceptual modes—the visual with the verbal, the verbal
with the aural, the visual with the linear, the numerical with the visual,
etc.; for the work is usually meant to be perceived not just in one
traditional way but, more likely, in a few ways. It could also be said
that I have endeavored, first, to synthesize my education in literature
and history with a growing interest in music and the visual arts and,
second, to test my inventive proclivities against the resistances of several unfamiliar media. This background may explain such idiosyncracies as why even my Constructivist Fictions, which are totally devoid of language, usually embody a strong narrative line, or why my
works seem at once so intellectual and so anti-intellectual; or why I
am more interested in results than in processes, or why I find myself
so often talking and writing about the work, and finally why this essay
is as it is.

One might also characterize my art as premeditated, impersonal, experimental and intelligent, although it eschews such traditional symp-
toms of how intelligence functions in art as allusions to past literature
and history. My works are particularly indebted, in different ways, to
such precursors as Moholy-Nagy and Theo van Doesburg, in addition
to my friends John Cage and Milton Babbitt; and I will gladly ac-
knowledge the influence of such earlier cultural movements as Con-
structivism, Dada and Transcendentalism, in addition to the "intermedia" developments of the past two decades. Except for my video
art, I have so far favored black and white as the sole colors indigenous
to art, believing that all other hues belong primarily to "illustration."

Though I once said that my creative work made me "a poet," I now
speak of myself as an "artist and writer," wishing there were in English
a single term that combined the two. "Maker" might be more appropriate, its modesty notwithstanding. The variousness of the total

work confuses not only the art public but also those critics who still expect someone to be just "a poet" or "a composer" or "a visual artist," rather than *all* of these things, and *much else* besides. On further thought, the principal problem with person-centered epithets such as "painter" and "writer" is that they become not descriptions but jails, either restricting one's creative activity, or defining one's creative adventure in terms of one's initial professional category (e.g., "artist's books"); for it should be possible for any of us to make *poems* or *photographs* or *music,* as we wish, and, better yet, to have these works regarded, plainly, as "poems" or "photographs" or "music." Perhaps the sum of my artworks is ultimately about the discovery of possibilities—not only in the exploitation of media but in art and, by extension, in oneself as a creative initiator.

Another reason for *my* discarding narrow terms is to suggest, if not insure, that the work as a whole be finally judged not just as Literature or just as Art but as something among and between; for it is only with my own kind, rare though they be, that I wish my total creative self ultimately to be compared. Perhaps the most accurate term for my imaginative endeavors would be "Language Art" and the most appropriate title for a retrospective exhibition would thus be *Wordsand.*

An earlier version of this essay appeared in *Interstate,* 8 (1976). In its present form, the essay will introduce the catalog to a traveling exhibition, *Wordsand,* that will begin at the Gallery of Simon Fraser Univ., Vancouver, B.C., in the Fall of 1978.

VISUAL LANGUAGE, VISUAL LITERATURE, VISUAL LITERACY

Clive Phillpot

The familiar words *literacy* and *numeracy* have more recently been joined by the word oracy, but when it comes to describing the skill of seeing (as opposed to looking) we seem to be stuck with the phrase 'visual literacy,' which suggests rather the skill of *reading* a pictorial image. One can, of course, see reasons for the coupling of these two words, but the absence of such words as 'visuacy' or 'pic-turacy,' or some similar verbal idiocy, still seems significant. The phrase *visual literacy* attests to the dominance of visual culture by the verbal. (In the beginning was. . . .)

While books of words allow one to conjure up often exotic pictures in one's mind, books of pictures do not necessarily conjure up corres-pondingly rich verbal accompaniments. Initially this seems to con-firm the supremacy of the verbal; however, paradoxically it might be said to attest to the power of the visual, in view of the comparative re-dundancy of the verbal. Perhaps it is also related to one's ability to ap-prehend a picture in an instant, rather than to the necessity of having to allow the passing of time in order to apprehend a text of similar complexity.

Although visual literacy may seem an inadequate term to describe the ability to see a picture, it seems not altogether inappropriate when applied to the ability to see/read visual or verbi-visual books. One might also employ the phrase *visual language,* in this connection, to suggest the possibility of sequential development of static visual images (thereby excluding animation, film, television, etc.).

In order to illustrate my assertion that the very phrase *visual liter-acy* is indicative of the dominance of the verbal culture, perhaps I might lapse into the first person singular for a while, since specificity might be the best way to convey my general drift.

I recently spoke in public of my remembrance of (or remembrance of the memory of) the time when I first read a book which had no pictures—no illustrations—and my sense of loss as I progressed through the book. I felt slightly embarrassed as I recounted this experience, and perhaps that is why I have thought more about it since.

Now I hold no particular brief for illustrators of pre-existing texts, rather the opposite, I remain to be convinced of their value—outside of decoration and punctuation, and the illustratively didactic. But one did have a different view as a child, illustrations seemed to be a natural element in storytelling; after all, one was reared first on pic-tures, then with pictures and words on equal terms. This did not mean, however, that one was incapable of liking or disliking illustrations, even declaring them good or bad.

The sense of loss, which I have referred to, was, however, part of growing up—growing out of picture books. But while I learned to accept the loss of pictures, the potency of the visual or verbi-visual was not to be denied. Enter the comics! There consequently existed for me, as a child, two kinds of 'reading' matter that never really met: books and comics. It was as if one read one kind of 'literature' with the left eye, and the other with the right. Another factor in this separation, beyond the different kinds of experience derived from books and comics, was the level of social acceptability of the two. I was conditioned into thinking that books of words were innately superior vehicles for the recreating of experience, rather than simply happening to be, in most cases.

For me books about modern art and artists were one source which helped to satisfy my need for visually stimulating books, after I outgrew comics; another was anthologies of the work of cartoonists such as Steinberg, Searle and François. Picture books became respectable again.

What I am trying to suggest is that I was developing at a time and in an environment in which verbal expression and exposition had been, and still were, clearly dominant over the visual, with few exceptions—one such being diagrams in school textbooks, for example. However, I was also growing up with the television age, though its dawning in my neck of the woods was rather late. This verbi-visual medium presented an increasingly potent alternative to books of words as it increased in its sophistication and in its grip on people's time, thereby also challenging the supremacy of the verbal. This development was paralleled by, and conceivably related to, the growth in the publishing of pictorial books for adults. Not just art books, but illustrated histories, visual encyclopaedias, travel books, pictorial biographies and so on. The potency of pictures was again being appreciated.

While comics and pictorial books are frequently published for the semi-literate, specifically as remedial reading aids, there are others which, because of the lack of imagination in their assembling, are a means for keeping readers semi-literate. Similarly the number of rewarding pictorial books published for the coffeetable market, excluding books which simply reproduce the work of good visual artists and photographers, is relatively low.

Visual language has been undervalued. It still is. But there has been a steady growth of interest in the sequential development of visual images. Serial imagery has been frequently highlighted in the visual arts in recent years, and not only in painting and sculpture, but also in the work of systemic/constructivist artists. A sizeable number of artists reared as painters and sculptors have also taken to making films and videotapes—on their own terms—another form of serial imagery. Finally, in this lightning and oversimplified tour of recent activity, we find visual artists making books, in tandem with the idea of discrediting the cult of the unique art object.

I have tried to help nudge along the idea of book art, whether visual or verbal, or both, over several years, because I was excited by the potential of what I had seen, since it seemed to me, dimly at first, to be the beginning of a recognition that books with visual, or verbi-visual, content could also be profound.

However, visual literacy (in the sense of fully apprehending the content of visual literature) still seems to me to be generally at a low level. The powerful emotional or intellectual potential of a string of static visual images in book form seems still not to be fully appreciated. It is possible that since purely visual images often convey a great deal of information simultaneously, and in a non-linear manner, that the linking of such images will always be susceptible to a variety of interpretations, some highly personal or idiosyncratic, because of the multiplicity of connections that can be made between complex single images. This being so, it may be impossible to convey in a visual book the experiential breadth of a novel, say, in the same number of pages. Perhaps it is necessary to compress these static images into a moving strip, the film or videotape, to convey as much. But while the lack of specificity of certain visual images makes visual literacy that much more difficult to attain, it also renders analogies with the novel somewhat suspect. The means to the same end—communication of experience and ideas, the shaking up of conventions, the affording of new insights, etc., etc.—are totally different. So that although the novel might therefore remain a convenient indication of what content can be packed between two covers, the normally linear means of the novelist will frequently be inappropriate to the visual artist.

In view of the capacity of almost any two people to communicate and interpret a substantial amount of information about each other, in a face to face encounter, before they even begin to speak, it must remain an open question as to whether visual books demand exceptionally visually literate reader-viewers. For it seems conceivable that certain books, given the right conditions or context, could communicate widely, if they are able to tap the innate level of visual literacy in us all, manifested in the ability to interpret body language, for example, even if only on a semi-conscious level.

Specific examples may help to support my view that visual languages are being developed which are not just word substitutes and that examples of book art, or visual literature, exist which indicate many fertile directions in which book art can develop.

I have singled out two books which, if described, may suggest some of the possibilities of the book form: *Loophole* by Telfer Stokes

and Helen Douglas (Weproductions, 11 Lady Somerset Road, London
NW5, England; 1975) and *Vulnerable Supplicant* by David Barton
(The Author, 45 Wellmeadow Road, London SE13, England; 1977).
I have chosen these two, first because I believe that both books use
the form to say something significant, and second because they use
different means, the former using photographic imagery, the latter
drawn images. Both books, as it happens, rely upon verbal language
in some measure, one indirectly, the other overtly—it is indeed argu-
able that the verbi-visual is potentially the most fruitful way forward
for book art. Both books are narrative in character, which gives them
a comprehensible form, and a beginning and an end (of sorts)—though
since they are visual books and less dependent upon sequentiality, it
is also a simple matter to flip back and retrace one's steps, or to get
sidetracked into eddies, echoes and parallels.

Loophole actually starts before it begins, since, once past the cover, one is given a glimpse of the composing of the beginning of the
book, and thereby reminded of the technical processes involved in
producing such a commonplace object—but not without some chican-
ery on the way. It also ends in a similar manner, but this time with
the camera slowly pulling away from the verso and recto of the last
page, revealing it juxtaposed with seven more of the last eight pages,
still laid out flat prior to folding and trimming.

In between one follows the visual narrative, the general form of
which resembles looping the loop, with a long drawn out conclusion
as one touches down and taxis to the end of the runway. The events
which occur generally drift across the shallow space of the book from
right to left when the double spread is used, so that the viewer is
drawn from left to right, from beginning to end. On reaching the high
point of the loop, one experiences a reversal of the visual sequence
with which the book commences. However, it is not just a question
of going to watch a film, and then seeing it run backwards, since
images which were carefully built up in the first sequence are literally
torn down in the second. At any time one is made aware of the page
of the book; the black and white photograph which, bled off, has become the page; and the events which have been photographed. Tran-
sitions between sequences are made through various forms of overlapping and interweaving. Rhythms other than the lateral movement
across pages are established. There is a sequence involving a sewing
machine, for example, in which the imagery is treadled up and down
the page, and another with a gramophone record where the imagery
revolves. There is also an occasion when one ventures, through a loophole, into a space beyond the page, which in turn also becomes the
book space.

While this book is almost entirely visual, the few words which appear are not without significance, even though they are inseparable

from the objects with which they are associated, such as a record label or a shop front. However, one's mental play with the visual images includes a verbal dimension which is reinforced by a series of chapter headings at the end of the book. One is reminded of puns ('Footnotes' as dancing footprints); one makes unwritten verbal connections between images.

Overall, one is made aware that sequences of visual images in book form are capable of mutely conveying a narrative which possesses an emotional, intellectual, even symbolic, function. Nevertheless, one's understanding of the meaning of the narrative seems to depend upon a largely intuitive response, after one has made the more superficial connections, though whether this is due to the multiple meanings and associations of the photographic images, or to one's level of visual literacy, is debatable.

Vulnerable Supplicant consists of pages of drawings accompanied by short pieces of writing, which aid one's understanding of the meaning of the narrative. However, as with *Loophole,* it, too, seems to demand an intuitive understanding beyond what is provided—in this case, by the prose as well as the information evident in the drawings themselves. In practically every other respect the two books are very unlike each other.

Vulnerable Supplicant is a selection from drawings made over a period of twelve years, which form a narrative, or progression, which commences with a drawing exercise, continues with some rather deliberate drawings, and progresses to a highly organic subtle style, which magically allows the depiction of insubstantial, highly mobile, images. The drawings are a little uneven, since their inclusion depends as much on their relevance to the narrative as their perfection as drawings; but there are some superbly evocative drawings, in which single lines suggest both outline and volume, space or solidity, suppleness or hardness. The artist is capable of describing, as if frame by frame, successive configurations of the mobile image which he can arrest at will in his mind's eye, so that the viewer, too, can follow and appreciate the evolving images.

As well as demonstrating the increasing skill of the artist in manipulating line, the book also documents the artist's exploration of his being. The words aid this process by making more specific the viewer's general understanding of the drawings; but, conversely, the text is made yet more poignant and moving by the organic changes in the drawings. Another tendency is for the drawings to begin to liberate themselves from dependence upon the text. The book commences with several pages of text, which perform the necessary task of sketching in the background to the series of drawings. Words also serve to pin down meaning throughout the book, but the later drawings stand substantially on their own, and become highly eloquent, in series, in their own right.

Neither of these books is a pamphlet, nor a one-idea booklet. Both are paperbacks which are not far from being physically acceptable, with regard to format and size, to a general bookseller, or to a public or school librarian, with the nerve to mix them in with commercially published paperbacks with a visual emphasis, say John Berger's *Ways of Seeing,* McLuhan's *The Medium Is the Massage,* or Saul Steinberg's *The Inspector,* or with visual poetry or photography. If this merging of book art with other kinds of visual books were to take place in such non-specialized and properly public places, books by artists would escape from the ghetto of 'artists' books,' and lose the last vestiges of the preciousness that they generally seek to reject. Otherwise, they will be condemned forever to be riders on the circle line of the art world, which, while not a fate worse than death, simply prevents them from reaching and stimulating a wider audience.

SELECTED BIBLIOGRAPHY

These are essays I would gladly have included here, had they not already been published before:

Apollinaire, Guillaume. "The New Spirit and the Poets," in Roger Shattuck, ed., *Selected Writings of Guillaume Apollinaire.* N.Y.: New Directions, 1949.

Arias-Misson, Alain. *"Poesia Visiva:* A Visible Poetry," *Chicago Review,* XXVI/3 (1974).

Ballerini, Luigi. "60 Years of Visual Writing," in *Italian Visual Poetry, 1912-1972.* N.Y.: Finch College Museum, 1973.

Bory, Jean-Francois. Introduction to *Once Again.* N.Y.: New Directions, 1968.

Boyles, Denis. *An Introduction to Design Poetics.* N.Y.: Assembling, 1976.

Carrion, Ulises. "The New Art of Making Books," *Kontexts,* 7-8 (1975).

Cobbing, Bob, and Peter Mayer. *Concerning Concrete Poetry.* London: Privately printed, 1976.

Colombo, John Robert. "A Found Introduction," in Ron Gross & George Quasha, eds., *Open Poetry.* N.Y.: Simon & Schuster, 1972.

Dencker, Klaus Peter. "Einleitung," *Text-Bilder Visuaelle Poesie International.* Koln: Verlag M. Dumont Schauberg, 1972.

Essary, Loris. Foreword to Ian Tarnman, *First Principles.* N.Y.: Future, 1978.

Gumpel, Liselotte. *"Concrete" Poetry from East and West Germany.* New Haven: Yale University, 1977.

Higgins, Dick. *George Herbert's Pattern Poems: In their Tradition.* W. Glover, VT: Unpublished Editions, 1977.

Hellerstein, Nina S. "Paul Claudel and Guillaume Apollinaire as Visual Poets: Ideogrammes Occidentaux and Calligrammes," *Visible Language,* IX/2 (Spring, 1975).

Houédard, Dom Sylvester. "Concrete Poetry & Ian Hamilton Finlay," *Typografica,* 8 (Dec., 1963).

Klonsky, Milton. Introduction to *Speaking Pictures.* N.Y.: Harmony, 1975.

Kostelanetz, Richard. "Words & Images Artfully Entwined," *Art International,* XIV/7 (Sept. 20, 1970).

—————. Introduction. *Imaged Words & Worded Images.* N.Y.: Outerbridge, 1970.

—————. "An ABC of Contemporary Reading," *Precisely: One* (Nov., 1977).

Kotik, Charlotta. Introduction to *Jiri Kolar: Transformations.* Buffalo: Albright-Knox, 1978.

Kriwet, Ferdinand. *Decomposition of the Literary Unit.* San Francisco: Nova Broadcast, 1971.

Marcus, Aaron. "An Introduction to the Visual Syntax of Concrete Poetry," *Visible Language,* VIII/4 (Autumn, 1974).

Mathews, Richard. "Intermedia Fictions and the Critical Consciousness," *Style,* IX/3 (Summer, 1975).

Mayer, Peter. "Poetics of the Alphabet," *Poetry Information,* 18 (Winter/Spring, 1977/78).

Mayor, David. "Book Art Digressions," *Artists' Bookworks.* London: Arts Council of Great Britain, 1975.

Millán, Fernando, & Jesús García Sánchez. "Prologo," *La escritura en libertad: Antología de poesía experimental.* Madrid: Alianza Editorial, 1975.

Moholy-Nagy, L. "Literature," *Vision in Motion.* Chicago: Theobald, 1947.

O'Donnell, Thomas E. "Maurice Roche: Crane, Carne," *Visible Language,* IX/2 (Spring, 1975).

Phillpot, Clive. "Book Art Digressions," *Artists' Books.* London: Arts Council of Great Britain, 1976.

Scherer, Jacques. *Le "Livre" de Mallarmé.* Nouvelle edition. Paris: Gallimard, 1977.

Schmidt, Siegfried J., ed. *Konkrete Dicktung: Texte und Theorien.* Munchen: Bayrischer Schulbuck Verlag, 1972.

Seaman, David. "Critical Problems with Concrete Poetry," *Point of Contact,* 5 (Summer, 1978).

—————. "The Development of Visual Poetry in France," *Visible Language,* VI/1 (Winter, 1972).

—————. "Renaissance Concrete Poetry and the Origins of a Visual Tradition in Literature," in Sophia Blaydes & Philip Bordinat, eds., *Selected Papers.* West Virginia University Foundation, 1976.

—————. "Typography and the Visual Poem," *Visual Language,* VI/2 (Spring, 1972).

Stott, William. *"Let Us Now Praise Famous Men," Documentary Expression and Thirties America.* N.Y.: Oxford Univ. Press, 1973.

Tatham, Campbell. "Mythotherapy and Postmodern Fictions: Magic is Afoot," in Michel Benamou and Charles Caramello, eds., *Performance.* Madison, WI: Coda, 1977.

Veres, Peter. Introduction to *The Argument of Innocence: A Selection from the Arts of Kenneth Patchen.* Oakland, CA: Scrimshaw, 1976.

Vree, Paul de. "Visual Poetry," in *Konkrete Poezie?.* Amsterdam: Stedelijk Museum, 1970.

Waldrop, Rosmarie. *Against Language?* The Hague: Mouton, 1971.

—————. "A Basis of Concrete Poetry," *Bucknell Review* (Fall, 1976).

Wallace, Ian. "Literature—Transparent and Opaque," in *Concrete Poetry.* Vancouver, B.C.: Univ. of British Columbia—Fine Arts Gallery, 1969.

Young, Karl. "Breakthrough Fictioneers," *Margins,* 7 (1973).

NOTES ON CONTRIBUTORS

JOHN M. BENNETT, born in 1942, describes himself as "Head, Luna Bisonte Prods, 137 Leland Ave., Columbus, OH 43214. Poet, conceptual writer, label maker, etc." He has also been a professor of Spanish literature. His recent publications include *Image Standards* (1975), *White Screen* (1976), *Do Not Cough* (1976), *Meat Watch* (1977), *Time Release* (1978), and *Contents* (1978).

GEOFFREY COOK, born in 1946, is a poet, critic, translator and artist. His translations of Catullus appeared a few years ago, and books of his presently in production include *The: A Book of Texts & Explanations* and *The Children of Marx & Coca Cola: The American Small Press in the 70's.* La Mamelle, the San Francisco polyarts complex, is publishing a micro-fiche edition of his visual poetry, *Vision & Revision.*

CHARLES DORIA, born in 1938, has taught classics at the University of Texas at Austin and both co-edited and co-translated the anthologies *Origins* (1976), *A Big Jewish Book* (1978) and *The Tenth Muse* (1978). Forthcoming collections of his own poems are *The Game of Europe* and *Austin Flaco.* He presently works in New York publishing.

LORIS ESSARY, born in 1946, co-editor of *Interstate,* has produced visual poetry, critical essays and theatrical pieces in Austin, Texas. He contributed a critical history of Assembling Press to *Assembling Assembling* (1978), and a book-length collection of his poems will appear soon.

RAYMOND FEDERMAN has been, by turns, Professor of French and Professor of English at SUNY-Buffalo. He edited the pioneering anthology *Surfiction* (1974) as well as writing and editing several critical books on Samuel Beckett; and his words appear in both English and French with equal facility and frequency. All but one of his visual fictions are discussed by Jerome Klinkowitz in these pages; that exception is the poster *Rumor Transmissable Ad Infinitum in Either Direction* (1976).

EUGEN GOMRINGER, born in 1924 in Cacheula Esperanza, Bolivia, founded the Eugen Gomringer Press in 1959 and has worked as an arts administrator in Germany and as an art director in Switzerland. He edited the anthology *Konkrete Poesie* (1972), and the most convenient collection of his own "concrete" poems is *Konstellationen/ Ideogramme/Stundenbuch* (1977).

ROLAND GRASS, born in 1926, is Professor of Foreign Languages and Literature and Assistant Dean of the College of Arts and Sciences, Western Illinois University. He is particularly interested in avant-garde art and literature at the beginnings of this century.

DICK HIGGINS, born in 1938, founded and directed the Something Else Press (1964-74). He recently published a critical history of *George Herbert's Pattern Poems: In Their Tradition* (1977) and is, he says, "presently writing a visual novel called *The Grid.*"

EMMA KAFELANOS took her doctorate in Comparative Literature at Washington University, St. Louis, and currently teaches it there. She writes that she is particularly "fascinated by the avant-garde of all periods, from Dada to the *nouveau nouveau roman.*"

JOHN JACOB, born in 1950, presently lives in Oak Park, IL. His latest book is a long poem entitled *Knee: Whip of Occasions.* He is presently working on some performance pieces and a group of stories which he describes as "a lot more conventional than things I did in the past."

JEROME KLINKOWITZ, born in 1943, is Professor of English at the University of Northern Iowa and the author of several critical books, including *Literary Disruptions* (1975) and his masterpiece, *The Life of Fiction* (1977). He recently completed two books, one about the sixties and the other about listening to jazz.

AARON MARCUS is currently Senior Lecturer at Bezalel Academy of Art and Design, Jerusalem, Israel. Born in Omaha, Nebraska, in 1943, he studied at Princeton and Yale, and then taught at Princeton, where he also directed the typographic workshop and the visual studies laboratory. His publications include *Soft Where Inc.,* a monograph devoted to his own work, and a special issue of the periodical *Visible Language.* The illustration accompanying his essay is his own "visual restatement of my article."

PETER MAYER is a lecturer in the Department of Visual Communication, School of Art and Design, at Goldsmith's College, University of London. In collaboration with Bob Cobbing, he compiled the privately printed, continually updated, inarguably invaluable bibliography, *Concerning Concrete Poetry* (34 Lanhill Rd., London W9 2BS, England).

HOLLY O'GRADY, raised in Duluth, MN, and educated at the University of Wisconsin—Madison, presently resides in New York City. While in Wisconsin, she was a contributing editor of *Midwest Art* and taught a course in criticism of the visual arts. Her own criticism has appeared, among other places, in *The Feminist Art Journal.*

CLIVE PHILLPOT, born in 1938, is a writer and art librarian who has worked in London and is presently at the Museum of Modern Art in New York. He has been involved with exhibitions of "Artists' Books" and has written on that subject for both exhibition catalogues and in magazines. He writes that he is "also interested in the application of

pigment to flat surfaces, as well as to surfaces which are not so flat,
and even in surfaces which are not flat at all."
BERN PORTER, born in 1911 and presently living in Salmond,
Maine, is a distinguished American man-of-letters. Books of his vis-
ual poetry include *Found Poems* (1972), *The Wastemaker* (1972) and
The Manhattan Telephone Book 1972 (1975).

JONATHAN PRICE, born in 1941, has taught Shakespeare and contemporary literature at several American universities. His books include *Lifeshow* (1973, co-authored), *Video Visions* (1977), and *The
Best Thing on TV* (1978). His major recent creative work consisted
of painting the *I Ching* on the abandoned West Side Highway in New
York City (1976), followed by a *Video I Ching.*

KEITH RAHMMINGS is a mysterious figure, rarely seen in New York,
even though he lives there, who edits *Blank Tape,* a periodical, out of
P.O. Box 371, Brooklyn, NY 11230.

STEPHEN SCOBIE is presently an Associate Professor of English at
the University of Alberta, Edmonton, and co-publisher-editor of the
critical periodical *Precisely.* Born in Scotland in 1943, he has resided
in Canada since 1965 and has written many articles about Canadian
and Scottish literature, in addition to several books of his own poetry.

DAVID W. SEAMAN, born in 1940, is Professor of French and chair-
man of the Humanities Division at Davis & Elkins College, Elkins,
WV. Since completing his doctorate on "French Concrete Poetry,"
(Stanford, 1970), he has contributed essays to *Visible Language* and
other magazines.

FRED TRUCK/BOLON DZACAB writes that he was "born in 1946
in the 9th layer of hell. His works include *Camping Out B, Tangerine
Universe in 3 Refrains,* and *The Polyp* (A Quetzalcoatl Production)
Tych, Polypytch Striking Camp. Most recently he has turned to illuminated manuscripts in multiple form."

KARL YOUNG, born in Kenosha, WI, in 1947, edits and usually
prints both the periodical *Stations* and the books of Membrane Press,
in Milwaukee, WI. His own poetry has appeared around the world,
and his critical essays have appeared in *Margins* and other magazines.

PAUL ZELEVANSKY, born in 1946, has authored *The Book of
Takes* (1976), a masterpiece of visual literature, and mounted exhibitions of his work with images, sounds and words around the U.S. His
current visual novel is tentatively titled "The Case for the Burial of
Ancestors," which he describes as a "21st Century illuminated manuscript disguised as a Great Book of the ancient world."

RICHARD KOSTELANETZ, born in New York, NY, in 1940, recently mounted at Simon Fraser University a retrospective of his work

with words, numbers and lines, as books, prints, drawings, audiotapes, videotapes and film, *Wordsand,* which includes an accompanying catalogue that collects his theoretical essays on these media. His recent publications include *One Night Stood,* a minimal novel; *Esthetics Contemporary,* an anthology; *Twenties in the Sixties,* previously uncollected essays on literature, criticism, thought and experience; *Constructs Two,* visual fictions; *Foreshortenings,* nonsyntactic prose; *Assembling Assembling,* an exhibition catalogue; and *Grants and the Future of Literature,* a polemical critique.

INDEX OF PROPER NAMES